# CHANGESCAPES

# CHANGESCAPES

## COMPLEXITY MUTABILITY AESTHETICS

## ROSS GIBSON

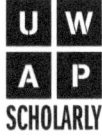

First published in 2015 by
UWA Publishing
Crawley, Western Australia 6009
www.uwap.uwa.edu.au

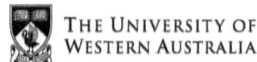
THE UNIVERSITY OF
WESTERN AUSTRALIA

This book is copyright. Apart from any fair dealing for the purpose of private study, research, criticism or review, as permitted under the *Copyright Act 1968*, no part may be reproduced by any process without written permission. Enquiries should be made to the publisher.

The moral right of the author has been asserted.

Copyright © Ross Gibson 2015

National Library of Australia Cataloguing-in-Publication entry

Creator: Gibson, Ross, 1956- author.

Title: Changescapes : complexity mutability aesthetics / Ross Gibson.

ISBN: 9781742587585 (paperback)

Subjects: Aesthetics.
    Art--Philosophy.
    Art appreciation.
    Multimedia (Art)
    Interactive multimedia.

Dewey Number: 701.17

Typeset in Bembo by J&M Typesetting
Printed by Lightning Source

# CONTENTS

| | | |
|---|---|---|
| Preface | | vii |
| 1 | Changescapes – An Introduction | 1 |
| 2 | Aqueous Aesthetics | 21 |
| 3 | The Rise of Multimedia Systems | 52 |
| 4 | Complex Dynamic Disciplines | 70 |
| 5 | The Known World | 77 |
| 6 | Attunement and Agility | 93 |
| 7 | Camouflage and Changefulness | 104 |
| 8 | Narrative Hunger – Geographical Information Systems, Google Street View and the Colonial Prospectus | 114 |
| 9 | Wayfaring Strangers: artistic investigations of the mood of dark tourism in online mapping | 134 |
| 10 | Ghosts of a Better Tomorrow: the volatile formalism of 1980s Film Workshop productions in Hong Kong | 147 |
| 11 | Cast Against Type | 161 |
| 12 | What the Eye Can Hear | 184 |
| 13 | A Forest. A Clearing. | 194 |
| 14 | Motility | 213 |
| 15 | Deep Water Time | 223 |

# PREFACE

This book examines various aesthetic forms that can be used for understanding complexity, changefulness, and aesthetic force. It draws on my past couple of decades making and analysing artworks concerned with these themes. To deepen the research, I have also spent a good deal of time looking at and writing about the work of other artists and authors who seem to be similarly fixated on the unfixed.

I have come to think of these aesthetic forms as 'changescapes'. By my definition, changescapes are peculiar artefacts or designed experiences – dynamic, tendency-governed, ever-reactive, never finished – that help us understand, accept and inhabit complexity. They dramatise change and afford us a clarified apprehension of it.

They are everywhere in contemporary culture: for example in forms of improvised music and social collaborations, in interactive and responsive multimedia installations, in adaptive simulation experiences, in responsive architecture and faux-ecological environments. They are everywhere because a heightened sensitivity to environmental dynamics and complexity is now everywhere.

What can these aesthetic forms – these 'changescapes' – teach us? How can we recognise them and best appreciate them? And how can we create them to their full potential so they can help us grasp better how instability and organisation play upon each other in our world of evolution and devolution?

Changescapes can be poems, databases, buildings, paintings, films, songs, designed environments, music, or artistic and scholarly careers interpreted as heuristic processes of proposition-and-response, meshing wilful humanity into stubborn reality and vice versa. Changescapes can help us know mutability by immersing us in it, by letting us be with it, contemplatively and therefore somewhat reflectively even as we remain within it. Change is the theme of these aesthetic forms and it is often their matter too, for they are usually comprised of fragile and ephemeral stuff that reacts to altering conditions in the larger world.

With changescapes, transformations happen at the boundaries – at the limits between the inside and the outside of their systems – and then the symptoms of change become manifest deeper inside them, so that mutability becomes palpably available for our consideration if we get amidst the situation. Such aesthetic forms have become plenteous recently because we are ready now to understand them and because we need now to understand mutability with them. We will ruminate on particular examples as we go through this book.

Versions of such aesthetic forms have been in human cultures for ages. In the Chinese shopping district of any sizable city around the world, for example, you will find a wonderful shop dedicated to 'live arts', where you can buy your supplies for aquariums, bonsai and water-fountains. Supplies for changescapes.

Then of course there is gardening, which is hardly a new enthusiasm.

Even so, for all the ancientness of these aesthetic responses to mutability, there is something about our present historical moment that is calling changescapes forth in greater numbers and greater variety. The book will try to grasp this 'something'.

As I say, this book comes after a couple of decades of my practical experimentation with changescapes. The artworks that I will describe and analyse are part of my professional research, in my role as an analyst of contemporary creative and cultural enterprises. My writing tries to capture, synthesise and communicate the main insights gleaned from these investigations, from my construction and immersion in these changescapes. By gathering several case studies – in many instances reflections on my own creations and the investigations of how well or otherwise they performed – I offer some concrete and personalized exemplifications and extensions of the more abstract or theoretical precepts that aerate the prose. And because my writing usually starts with reflection on direct experience and experiments, the prose in these chapters often has a witnessing voice and a personal tone. I hope this brings immediacy rather than self-indulgence to the ideas that are put to work and put under a glass here.

I hope too that I am able to show that you cannot know much about complex circumstances unless you are attentive both to your own entangled perspectives and to your own unfurling experiences within those dynamic systems. Moreover because emergent systems cannot be frozen and regarded as finished objects, and because they cannot be understood as separate or critically distanced from my own immersed self *while still being the emergent event-things that I am trying to know*, personal accounting is in fact an essential aspect of the quest to understand the quickness and mutability within the protean phenomena that attract my attention. Hence the first-person voice in many of these essays.

So by mixing the particular and the general modes of address – the case studies and the theories – I hope to generate some fresh understanding of our changeful contemporary culture, with all its complexity, with all its demands on our personal immersion and continuous, dynamic engagement. I hope to tune in to the volatility that characterises this world of ours where, as Ralph Waldo Emerson wrote in another time and place, 'every end is a beginning' and 'there is always another dawn risen on the mid-noon'.[1]

## Notes

1   Ralph Waldo Emerson, 'Circles' in his *Essays: First Series*, first published 1841, Project Gutenberg E-book, Release Date: 1-12-2008, p. 135. http://www.gutenberg.org/files/2944/2944-h/2944-h.htm

# 1

# CHANGESCAPES – AN INTRODUCTION

I once spent some wondrous months in the Pilliga Scrub, a vast scree of native Australian forest gone feral in northwest New South Wales. I was working with John Cruthers, Joel Peterson and Eric Rolls, grafting a film out of Eric's marvelous vast scree of a book, *A Million Wild Acres*.[1]

One afternoon Eric took me unusually deep into the forest, proffering the chance to meet a white man we will call Muller, whom I had heard about and whom Eric had met a couple of times. The summer day had been parching, breezeless mostly, except for some flukey little gusts and spiralling willy-willies that haggled with the Land Rover whenever we broke out of the foliage-cover and traversed a clearing. But by the time we got close to Muller's compound, the sun was dropping and some humid clouds had climbed out of the river-junction not far away. Before long, light rain was spritzing the dusty pines and eucalypts, releasing into the air a welcome round tang that soothed the soft palate like a lozenge.

Eric drove around for a bit, doing that directional divining of corrugated tracks that mystifies anyone new to the Pilliga. Finally we pulled up at a walking track and ventured in. Ten minutes from the road, we came upon a clearing bounded on all sides by stacked short bolts of timber that were commercially useless but aesthetically thrilling, with their patterns of knotty convolutions and sappy striations presenting all the colours of blood in sculptural arrays aligned in every which way as if to give shifting volume and spectral tone to the gloaming air. Eric called out several times: a few words, including Muller's full name, but mostly variants of coo-ee noises that were more like birdcalls or the creaking of timber, as if he was loath to startle the place with too much human intrusion. But all was quiet, deserted right now except for us, so incursive and curious.

I remember padding around the compound awe-struck, alarmed by the noise my boots were generating in the red gravel. I recall calculating how it would have taken one man maybe several thousand mornings of work to make just the timber stacks in this 'installation', let alone all the other details of the place. And I recall thinking that this must be all Muller does: tend and change the place every day.

The compound had been a timber-mill once but it had undergone some slow metamorphosis, till now it was a devotional kind of site. Devotional to what, I still can't say exactly, but devotional all the same. For it could have been sustained in this serene appearance only by dint of a devoted lifetime spent designing and laboriously adjusting and maintaining. And a good stint of custodial labour had occurred recently. For the entire clearing – about half the size of a cricket field – had been raked so the ground was free of footprints and was linearly pulsating with confluences of curves and rectangular tracts that seemed to be mustering the breezes in cooling little arabesques all around us.

At least, the compound had been free of footprints till we had blundered in. Which makes me think the raking was not only one of the most beautiful aesthetic configurations I have ever seen but also some sly and leery method of surveillance.

## Changescapes – An Introduction

I couldn't resist exploring, all the time listening for other footfalls and the noise of a rifle cocking. Near the northeast of the clearing, zinging with a keen sensory acuity that had been stimulated by the mystery and the delicacy of the place, I ventured over to a covered contraption. It was a timber structure that I can best describe as an log-entablatured shelter roughly assembled but also distinguished with proportions and a style worthy of epithets like 'minimalist' and 'Zen'. Inside, an old wheel-less truck was installed on blocks. From the truck's unimpeded back axles several heavy drive-belts extended in different directions across the graveled compound, connecting to blade-benches and saw-pits. Evidently you could start the truck, slip it into gear and thereby have an entire sawmill humming and zinging, complete with a feature whereby one driver-belt conveyed sawdust out to a fragrant disposal-pit on the southern edge of the site.

Panning to the left, I noticed there was a small wooden shack nearby. Well, it was more like a roofed box two metres long, one metre wide, the height of a man standing. Peering through the door, I saw that it was an enclosed bed, empty right now but installed there at the centre of the compound, insulated from intrusion by sixty paces across the crunchy gravel on all sides. From the bed, I had a direct sightline to the main saw-pit and out to the sector of the perimeter where Eric and I had ventured in. Alongside the bed, a car battery was connected to a radio that sprouted a high-wire aerial, hand-made, Calder-esque and pivot-able to catch a full dome of transmission in the huge sky.

As the sun waned, I had time to discover just one more detail. Out on the western boundary of the clearing, behind a thin stand of gum trees, there was another simple structure that you could barely see from the precinct-proper. It was a smaller version of the construct that housed the truck. As I closed in on it, I could see that it was a kind of miniature temple. Suspended from the rafters or balanced on plinths made from logs, there were maybe thirty 'relics' of the forest – startling things, some of which might have been macabre except that each object's relative placement and scale and particular qualities all mitigated systematically against repulsion. It was a wondrous and reverent array. There was a delicate skeleton of a small marsupial coiled as if about to spring back to fleshy life; there was a large split rock, a metre across, showing a fossilised fern-print; plus a melted black bakelite telephone; the bonnet mascot of an old Chevrolet; a shiny clean skull that might have been of a cat but was larger than any domestic feline I'd ever seen. All these things were displayed like treasures the forest had yielded to a dutiful fossicker. The collection was strange, but special.

Devotional. That word came to me again. The roofed structures I'd found were like emotional compression-chambers. Their placement, their volume, their material, their contents, the counterpoint between the cool grey light inside and the sharper brightness outside: all these features rendered each structure into a compressed zone that intensified a particular emotional charge within a larger compound which was already extraordinarily atmospheric, so deliberately rarefied and intensified in comparison to the rest of the forest.

I remember marvelling at how dextrously Muller had made and located these three aesthetic 'power-plants' – the truck-shelter, the sleeping box and the reliquary – inside the bigger force-field of his raked and wood-stacked compound. He knew something about rhythm, about establishing and off-setting frames in space, matter and time; he knew how to manage bounds that counterposed relaxation and tension, vacuity and intensity, downbeat and upbeat, the one side and the other side. There was something about wildness and domesticity in there too, nature and culture itching at each other. These thoughts undulated in me as I day-dreamed in the reliquary.

Back at the edge of the clearing, Eric whistled. Having installed himself on a stump near one of the woodstacks, he had been jotting in his notebook, taking care to be less of a sticky beak than I had been. He called out that he was keen to go and find the way out of the forest before all the light was gone.

As we trudged to the walking path, I turned for one last view of the site. In wide-shot I could see how the record of our visit was footprinted all over the clearing. As stark as a CCTV report, there was the single track that Eric had made over to his tarrying spot and there was the record of everything I had inspected, evidence of how snoopy I had been, where I had come in and out of the compound, how I had breached its porous boundary, brought my strangeness in and bandied it about.

Driving back to our base camp in the last half-hour of evening, we could smell recent burning. The tasty aroma of damp ash. Now and then we could see where a gentle fire had knocked back some of the undergrowth but had not taken to the trees. Eric noted the peculiarities of the burning pattern. When we merged on to a larger track we came upon a Forestry Department truck. As is usual in the bush, we stopped for a chat, keeping the engine running. No, they had not done any burning; they were on the way back from road maintenance, as the small 'bobcat' grader on the trailer behind the truck testified. 'Hmmph, funny,' said Eric. 'Yeah, funny,' said one of the Forestry blokes, who then bunted his truck out of neutral and waved a gesture as they beetled off, as if to say funny's just ordinary.

I was intrigued and didn't calm down overnight. Next morning I badgered Eric to go back after lunch.

This time we tooted the Land Rover's horn as we approached the pedestrian path and once we were walking, Eric coo-eed ahead. When we got to the edge of the clearing, Muller was standing there, his single line of footprints graphic against the freshly raked ground of the entire compound. He was spry, strong, smelly. Maybe sixty-five years of age, but this was indiscernible, truly. He was plainly suspicious, not to say hostile, until Eric spoke and explained how they'd met years before and how they had a couple of mutual acquaintances in town. Muller relaxed a tad, unclenched his jaw and started talking quickly in a soft brogue that was 'country Australian' but sometimes had Irish and sometimes German patterns in it. We asked a couple of times if he had any objection to our filming. He hefted the camera, cocked an ear to listen to its whirring, showed some interest in the vinyl dust-cover, and made no objection.

After attuning myself to his morse-code verbiage, I understood that a forestry fella had told him this morning that there had been strangers about, but he knew this much from the footprints: two strangers, who'd never been here before, yes you two. Eric explained how we were interested in the history of the forest and how I'd been fascinated by his mill. I added that I thought his mill was beautiful. Muller registered that I was genuine, but it was clear the 'beauty' topic was not going to sway him much. I added that I was wanting to understand how everything that had happened in the forest was still producing effects there, still hanging around the place.

This seemed to light him up. He quipped, 'Ghosts, you mean.' Not really a question. 'Kind of', I replied. And he was off. He talked at pace about how he would see things sometimes at night and how the radio tells him stuff you would not expect it to. Outside of the specific environment we were standing in, this might have been crazy talk, and clearly he was living a hard life, but it seemed prissy to judge him by any standards I had walked in with. He was functioning in a place that remains aesthetically unmatched in my experience – except perhaps for some gardens in Kyoto – and he was devoted to it somehow. Sustained by it too, not in body so much as in whatever spirit or mania drove him along day by day.

Once Muller had finished his ghost monologue, I seemed to have licence to ask him more questions. Most of the time he ignored them and I noticed that he had no censoring sieve between thinking and speaking. Living alone out here (by Eric's calculations Muller had been here for more than forty-five years since first leaving the closest town to take over the family mill when he would have been in his late teens) … living alone out here he had probably always let his thoughts get vocalised as they formed. Decades of solitude had led to this: he did not talk to himself so much as he told the place what he was thinking. Anyway, one of my questions elicited a short, lucid response. When I asked him why he continued to work so hard every day making this cache of lumber that he plainly never made any attempt to sell, he said that the forest is always offering timber ready for cutting. I asked him about the fires we saw yesterday. He wondered out loud if I ever speak much to the Forestry fellas. I responded I never run into them, except for yesterday, which was not at all normal, and besides, I don't live around here. He countered with a long stream of consciousness, within which there was some information to the effect that yesterday afternoon he had lit out from the compound when the clouds had come up because it was a good chance to do some firing in a nearby tract that needed some heat in it, because he was confident that the rains would come down with the sunset to contain the burn exactly as it had to go.

I was keen to get him talking more about this, for he had some fire-farming knowledge and an ecological philosophy. But he wanted to start the truck and cut some timber. So that is what happened.

He got the mill going. And it was beautiful. By which I mean there was an elegance and a design to it all, a sense of its rightness in cohesion offset by enigmas that drew you back to consider it repeatedly. In operation the mill was loud, acrid and dangerous too. But it *was* beautiful. Muller had made it so. Or at least it had become so as a consequence of how he had immersed himself in the place, in the feedback patterning of action and reaction amongst the trees over extensive time.

The blades kept humming and more bolts of timber stacked up. Until after a while, Muller mentioned to no-one in particular that he was keen for us to go now, and it would be good if we didn't come back. Which seemed fair enough to me. So I've never re-visited. Except often in my memory and sometimes in dreams, where the compound grows evermore vivid and telling.

Muller features for a few minutes in the film we made but I know I have never found the right context to bear witness to what I think is so significant about him. Straight away, I have to emphasise that these are just my interpretations, perhaps my projections. As far as I could tell, Muller himself cared not one bit about his meaning or about how a stranger might use his mill for rhapsodies and theories. He had no explicit thesis, no evident need for a reader or an audience. He was no local reincarnation of Henry David Thoreau. But he built his compound. It was rigorous and eloquent. And it means something.

I have thought about it all these years and I am just now getting a better grasp of how remarkable it was, that clearing in that forest. Muller's compound and my encounter with him prompted my notion of the 'changescape', this idea I have that there are long-established aesthetic systems that are built purposefully to intensify our experience and to enhance our understanding of the complex dynamics that are at play when our natural, social, technological and psychological domains commingle and alter each other in this world that is full of mutability. Like Muller's mill, a changescape is something predominantly aesthetic rather than pragmatic. Productive of understanding primarily, a changescape is designed to produce cognitive and sensorial wealth rather than material profit. A changescape helps you think and feel so that you are *engaged* with the flux-infused world, so that you feel informed about that world's maintenance and motivated by its momentum rather than distressed by its entropy.

Muller's clearing was a superb aesthetic system whose matter, method and formal arrangements illuminated the themes of the fragility, mutability and fecundity of the world. The mill was an exemplary changescape, therefore, a predominantly meditative, albeit laborious construct that was internally maintained and always evolving in concert with a dynamic environment that pressed in from outside. By dint of daily work and thoughtful, adaptive design within the compound, and by occasional assertions and exertions (the fire-farming and the relic-fossicking, for examples) out in the surrounding environment, Muller produced a complex aesthetic expression of the cohesive energies and the disruptive instabilities that entangled the forest, himself and his compound cosseted in the clearing.

The mill was a zone for intensified perception, reflection and conception. And for me it has produced some slow-burn understanding, if not a quick revelation.

Muller marked an edge against predominant, primary energies (which we can call 'nature') and he produced a system of prevalent design (which we can call 'culture'). He worked always with the fact that his creation was brittle. He knew that he must constantly improvise reiterated and ever-modifying actions and reactions to keep the compound composed. He knew that alterations come in unbidden from 'nature' as weather, as windborne seeds, swooping birds and foraging animals, as fire, as human intruders like us and the forestry fellas. And from all this contentious pushing and pulling of knowledge, power, impotence and ignorance, he fashioned a living, habitable meditation on his patterned but unstable place in the world.

Muller's clearing has helped me understand better how the edges between culture and the cosmos are porous and how startling pulses of energy surge within and across us so that everything at any one moment is unlike the instant before, even though historically determined tendencies also govern the continuing cohesion of the physical and psychological entities we are and the cultural systems we have made. Muller must have known this too, at some level, when (as his family in town attested somewhat wearily) he stopped selling the wood and fashioned the mill into an aesthetic thing, changing it from its original economic function. So much hard work must have been founded on a belief or a philosophy. Otherwise, why toil so ardently when money was not the issue? At some stage he ceased being a miller and became a changescaper.

A changescaper is more concerned with *systems* than *structures*. A structure is founded on the permanence and solidity of its constituent parts and joints, whereas a system is a set of contingent relationships evolving, shifting while also persisting through time. A structure is solid-state and mechanistic, deployed against devolution; whereas a system is fluid, in slippery balance with mutability. A system finds its balance – internal and external – when the several simultaneous modes of its action, information, remembrance and alteration all manage to moderate each other for the purposes of its survival within the larger host environment. And a system becomes a changescape when all this complexity is marshalled by deliberate human care for mainly contemplative or aesthetic ends rather than pragmatic purposes.

When something is 'aesthetic' – by dictionary definition, the aesthetic is that which is 'perceptible by the senses' – it is taken out of the explicitly functional realm and offered in the service of contemplation, for appreciation first by the stimuli gathered and gauged by the nervous system, and then by intellection.[2] Which leads to another definitive characteristic of changescapes: so they can be informed by the most comprehensive array of intensively-felt sensations, changescapes require your presence in them. This sense of presence is attained preferably your physical immersion in the space-time configurations that the changescape presents. A changescape ignites your sensorium first and then your cerebellum; you enliven it with your presence so that the instabilities you cause in it become fascinating, informative and somewhat constitutive of the system. You and your actions and the reactions of the systems over time are all part of the changescape. A changescape works best not only when you are inside it but also when you know it inside yourself somehow, when you know it because of what you can 'grasp' with your inquisitive bodily senses as they get cross-referenced against the reflection furnished by your memory and the projections furnished by your imagination. Thus a good changescape can stimulate the interplay between your sensation and your cerebration; it can prompt in you and for you a nervy investigation of space, time, energy and self spanning the present, the past and the future all at once. You can use a good changescape to feel the options as well as the obligations presented by its activeness and reactiveness; you can use a good changescape to speculate about possibility in a world of uncertainty. So a good changescape is a system you can use to contemplate dynamics, to be with complexity more effectively.

In Paul Cilliers' lucid study *Complexity and Postmodernism* – a study that we will reach for several times in chapters to come – he explains that 'complexity is diverse but organised' and that 'descriptions of it cannot be reduced to simple, coherent and universally valid discourses'. To know a system, it's best to describe it. And 'to describe a system,' he observes, 'you have … to *repeat* the system', paradoxically accepting that with each new iteration it will have moved on and become different.[3] You cannot reduce a complex circumstance to a simplified model or to stabilised rules, requirements and expectations. For complexity is definitively dynamic, relationally intricate, contingent on other altering factors, and always evolving. You need to *experience* a complex circumstance, to be with its changes through time, to feel its shifts whilst also being attuned to the historically determined tendencies and feedback patterns of stimuli and responses that maintain organisation within it. Or as Cilliers explains, 'complex systems have to grapple with a changing environment … To cope with these demands the system must have two capabilities: it must be able to store information concerning the environment for future use; and it must be able to adapt … when necessary.'[4]

In traditional artforms, this sense of complexity and the concomitant need to attend to adaptability is often evoked by means of absences carefully implanted by the artist so that the perceiver's imagination is spurred to provide options for the completion of the work. Or in a related but different strategy, patterns of ambiguity and excesses of plausible meaning are provided by the artist so that various canny interpretations – all contextually charged and valid yet mutually unresolvable – contend for the appreciator's acceptance. William Empson's *Seven Types of Ambiguity* is the classic study of aesthetic and semantic plenitude in literature.[5] More recently, Andrew Benjamin's investigation of the phenomenon of 'incompletion' in painting has added to our understanding of the importance of an organised kind of 'restlessness' in an artwork.[6]

In artforms like literature and painting, therefore, the adaptability and complexity can occur in an abstract kind of space between the perceiver's self and the artwork, in the strummed intellect, memory and senses of the person engaging with the work under scrutiny at any particular instant. In more recent times, by contrast, digital-computational systems have emerged that enable the artwork itself – not just the relationship between the work and the perceiver – to transmogrify in response to shifting contexts and behaviors shared by the artwork and the appreciator. Influencing and influenced by the active and activating codes written into the artwork, the appreciator is participant within the work, not scrutinising it at an exquisite, evaluative distance. (For me the pre-eminent examples are still some of the early classics such as Gary Hill's immersive, multimedia environment 'Tall Ships' and Char Davies' emergent moodscape 'Osmose'.) In such artworks the adaptability and complexity are to be found in the active and reactive potentialities of the work as well as in the imaginative 'space' between the perceiver and the work. Rather than only being implicit and always somewhat opaque inside the ruminations of each perceiver, the play of relationships and repercussions that get activated by the perceiver's engagement with an interactive-immersive environment can now also be made explicit and somewhat observable by others who are also in the work itself. Whether or not these digital innovations necessarily make for an enhanced aesthetic or intellectual experience, well, that debate continues alive and aloud.

The drive to understand the dynamics of emergent circumstances is strengthening in contemporary culture, as evinced not only in the preponderance of immersive artworks but also in the popularity of computational gameplay. And then there is the proliferation of simulation systems used for entertainment as well as for training in sports, medicine, aviation or emergency services, to name just a few of the most innovative domains.[7] All of which brings us back to Paul Cilliers' thesis about the most effective ways to understand what occurs inside the 'constrained diversity' that agitates complex experiences.[8] Instead of producing a schematised blueprint of complexity, Cilliers asserts, you need to get inside the system, adopting as many vantage-points as possible so as to generate *an interrelated set of narratives* that help you inspect and then speculate about the endless variability of the system. You have to propose 'what if' scenarios, cross-referencing the potentialities of the situation against your own history and against the accounts of action and reaction that have already coursed through the system. Thus you can *get a feeling* for the way the system is tending. As fuzzy as this sounds, it is true to the workings of complexity, and it is the best one can hope for, no matter how much one might wish to model the system and find invariant principles that would allow you to predict the behaviors unfurling. For there is no way around the fact: when faced with complexity, predictive thinking is just wishful thinking.

'Complex systems are open systems' writes Cilliers. Their constituent parts (including yourself, if you are amidst them) and their dominant actions all change from moment to moment, which means often 'the very distinction between "inside" and "outside" the system becomes problematic'.[9] Complexity is not especially tractable to analysis, therefore, because the 'object' under analysis is altering from moment to moment, changing its objective qualities instant by instant. In Cilliers' words, 'a complex system is not constituted merely by the sum of its components, but also by the intricate *relationships* between those components'.[10] If we try to map those relationships as an active network, 'any given narrative will form a path, or trajectory, through the network … [and] as we trace various narrative paths through it, it changes'. If we were to 'cut up' a complex system, we would find that our 'analytical method destroys what it seeks to understand'.[11]

This aligns well with my concept of changescapes which, like Muller's compound, are engrossing, puzzling, active, reactive, systematic, endless. Changescapes encourage contemplative engagement with mutability. They are lively, which is not to say they are necessarily *live*, although they can be, as in the case of great gardens or aquaria.

Therefore changescapes are 'Romantic' in the original and radical sense, as witnessed in William Wordsworth's 'The Tables Turned':

> Our meddling intellect
> Mis-shapes the beauteous forms of things:–
> We murder to dissect.[12]

Changescapes are not anti-intellectual; they are extra-intellectual, nimble, cross-disciplinary and curious about the paradoxically unstable 'status' of the world. Dynamic and predominantly aesthetic, they are concerned with perception arising through all available senses, perception evolving through inquisitive immersion in the experience that must be understood. They require the readiness that Wordsworth celebrates:

> Come forth, and bring with you a heart
> That watches and receives.[13]

Or as Samuel Taylor Coleridge proposed, there is a way to make art based on 'intuitive apprehension'. The idea is glossed by Sherman Paul in his ingenious study of Romanticism:

> [For the Romantics,] intuitive apprehension ... was man's creative power, the warrant of his freedom. Not only did its synthesising powers account for the way in which experience becomes meaningful, but being an imaginative faculty as well, it could directly seize reality. And this apprehension of reality, though mystical in the epistemological sense of making the knower one with the thing known, was not the vaporous emotional state usually ascribed to mysticism; it was a cognitive experience, the liberating power of which came from possessing Ideas.[14]

William Empson's famous analysis of the profuse yields in Gerard Manley Hopkins' 'The Windhover' is a good example of intuitive apprehension circulating via text between writers (in this case both Hopkins and Empson) and readers. By the time Empson has shown us the plenteous ways the poem can buckle, pirouette and take evocative flight, it is clear we are examining a changescape, an aesthetic system that helps us apprehend restlessness.[15]

Some of the newest developments in aesthetic form – those facilitated by computers and digital systems of sound, vision and text – are clearly being used by artists to develop better comprehension of the changefulness in complexity. David Rokeby is one of the canniest practitioners in this field. Being simultaneously an artist and a theorist, Rokeby is both creatively inside and reflectively outside the systems he is trying to know. He contends that complexity and its dynamics are best understood through *interaction*, defined as a means by which the artist contrives to 'reflect the consequences of our actions or decisions back to us'. 'Rather than creating finished works,' Rokeby observes, 'the interactive artist creates relationships'.[16]

I would add that because these artworks and their relationships are not entirely controlled or securely bounded when each new interaction by a participant brings fresh elements into the system, the artworks are always becoming something *other* than (but related to) what they were a moment ago. But they are more than chaotic or entropic. They are designed by the artists to be heuristic, to encourage exploration and discovery. As Rokeby explains, such artworks are 'havens of safe interaction'; they are places and processes in which, contemplatively but also actively, the participant can be with and understand change.[17] They perform *explicitly* as changescapes therefore, enhancing in their interactive participants an improvisational capability and helping them live without pre-set and permanent principles. Forget the faith in Platonic ideals. Cue the play of contingency in algorithms or underlying codes.

Changescapes are not products. They are more like *projects* or *processes*, because they are made by, through and for the continuous dynamics that get established between themselves and their perceivers. When they help us understand our existence in a world of unremitting change, they tend not to finish.

I've used the notion of 'understanding' several times already. It seems a simple enough word. It describes the results of acknowledgement: to stand under an experience, to be covered by the experience. It is an aesthetic process. You conceive of the pertinent elements by first receiving and perceiving them all relationally and systematically, through the several channels of your integrated senses. (The French word for 'understand' is 'comprendre' – to *take* [prendre] this *with* [com] that, to grasp something, to bring it in close to you by integrating its component elements into one aggregation not separated from you.) Furthermore, understanding is immersive and reiterative. You comprehend an experience cumulatively, by bringing it close, delving into it and being inundated by it repeatedly whilst also reflecting on it. Being inside and simultaneously outside.

Through the interactive collection of understanding, complexity can be comprehended incrementally, continuously, until one 'has the feeling', 'gets with the program' or 'is tuned in'. Changescapes get made, maintained and understood this way.

Which is how this book will proceed. Mostly it will offer a series of reports from within particular changescapes that I have tended. Both implicated and reflective, the book will be a kind of participant-observer's memoir about my productions and my reflective critiques of interactive-immersive environments. In this respect, I take some guidance from Henry David Thoreau's famous paradox: his clearing at Walden Pond was both detached from and immersed in the phenomena of nature and society that he yearned to understand. Or as he wrote in his diary on November 1858: 'You cannot see anything until you are clear of it'; and as he showed so vividly at Walden, you cannot sense anything unless you are steeped in it.[18]

Because complex systems have histories which determine the tendencies that brace the systems against changefulness at every present moment, any study of them must also pause now and then to 'read memory', to align the interpretations of present culture with the momentum bequeathed by past cultural forms.

## Changescapes – An Introduction

Or to borrow Thoreau's notion of 'doubleness' again, one needs to be able to zoom back and forth instantaneously within a depth of field that connects the past with the present and with the imminent so that one perceives patterned continuities operating in concert with change.

My intuition, which this book assays, is that well-designed changescapes can reveal systematic relationships that help us understand the way of the world. The way of a world where, as Ralph Waldo Emerson envisaged it, 'there is no sleep, no pause, no preservation, but all things renew, germinate and spring'.[19] By steeping ourselves in changescapes and also getting reflectively clear of them reiteratively, we might understand some of our everyday complexity. By increments we might get a better feeling for our place in the world and for our roles in its restless processes, which are simultaneously vegetative and entropic, never static when viewed across a significant span of time.

I first grasped this intuition in Muller's compound. I got a feeling for the vitality of contemplative environments. Meditative places. Systems that hold us while they also fold us into the built but ever-unbuilding spaces and systems that constitute experience. The subject of this book.

### Notes
1. Ross Gibson, director, John Cruthers, producer, *Wild*, 1993, 16 mm film, 54 minutes duration, distributed by Ronin Films, Canberra; Eric Rolls, *A Million Wild Acres: two hundred years of man and an Australian forest*, Melbourne: Nelson, 1981.
2. G.A. Wilkes and W.A. Krebs (eds), *Collins English Dictionary* (3rd edition), Sydney: Harper Collins, 1991, p.24.
3. Paul Cilliers, *Complexity and Postmodernism*, p. 130 and 10 respectively.
4. Cilliers, p. 10.
5. William Empson, *Seven Types of Ambiguity*, second edition, London: Chatto and Windus, 1947 (first published 1930).

6   See throughout Andrew Benjamin, *Disclosing spaces: on painting*, Manchester: Clinamen Press, 2004.
7   For a quick view into the contemporary cultures and businesses developing and utilising simulations, see the websites of peak bodies such as Simulation Australasia and the Society for Modeling and Simulation International.
8   Cilliers, p. 127.
9   Cilliers, p. 99.
10  Cilliers, p. 2.
11  Cilliers, p.130, p. 2.
12  William Wordsworth, 'The Tables Turned' (1798) in T. Hutchinson and E. de Selincourt (eds), *Wordsworth: Poetical Works*, London: Oxford University press, 1936, p. 377.
13  Wordsworth, p. 377.
14  Sherman Paul, *The Shores of America: Thoreau's inward exploration*, Chicago: University of Illinois Press, 1958, p. 5.
15  See the seventh of Empson's ambiguities. Consider, also, the similarities between the prevailing tendencies that animate and govern complex systems, on the one hand, and the 'inscape' that Hopkins believed holds 'instressed' phenomena together in the exalted world, on the other hand.
16  David Rokeby, 'Transforming Mirrors: subjectivity and control in interactive media', in Simon Penny (ed.), *Critical Issues in Electronic Media*, Albany: State University of New York Press, 1995, p. 133 and p. 152,
17  David Rokeby, 'The Construction of Experience: interface as content', http://www.davidrokeby.com/experience.html accessed 25-03-15.
18  F. Garber, *Thoreau's Redemptive Imagination*, New York University Press, 1977, p. 2.
19  Ralph Waldo Emerson, 'Circles' in his *Essays: first series*, first published 1841, Project Gutenberg E-book, Release Date: 1-12-2008, p. 143. http://www.gutenberg.org/files/2944/2944-h/2944-h.htm

# 2

# AQUEOUS AESTHETICS

### Prelude

I am embarrassed to say how long it has taken me to sense the ocean-like qualities of human culture in my part of the world. I have an explanation, which is not an excuse: as a descendent of gardeners and potters from the border country south of the Scottish lowlands, I have always been encouraged to understand culture as something definitively grounded. Placed. Located. Moreover I grew up in landlocked suburbs in Australia, which is seemingly the most earthed and earthy of continents. Where I lived as a youngster, the options always appeared to be just threefold, all land-related: (a) you could tell stories about your *arising* from the ground that sustains you (which would make you Aboriginal); or (b) you could tell stories about your *arriving* at landfall (which would make you a migrant), or (c) you could broker some alliance between these roles (which would make you contemporary and maybe some avant-garde kind of patriot).

Whichever role you chose or were given, you were meant to dig in and get settled. Not for Australians the stories of metamorphosis, drift and fluid emergence, for example, that once energised the Greeks in pre-Socratic times, when Thales and Heraclitus proclaimed that everything and everyone stems from water and that no river holds its form till next you step into it.[1] Why should I think about drifts and dynamics as if they meant anything to my culture? Australia is, after all, the place where the land is definitive. Rock solid. 'Country tells us who we are': Indigenous Australians have said this to us interlopers ever since the tall ships arrived.

In my part of the world settlers have been slow to comprehend how country can undulate and flow, how there is a recursive and ever-evolving dynamic within it. In other words, *settlement* is not the only action you can or should perform in country. Status can get untethered in country. *Dynamics* can define a place too. So there is sky country in Australia, and river country, water country, estuary country, ocean country, as well as the more familiar tracts of more or less solid earth.[2] These are places that are best understood as endless events rather than as locations or settings; places that can be fluid or airy or ethereal and constantly altering while also being structured and ready for coherence. (Doubtless this is not such a new idea to people from, say, volcanic and earthquaken geographies. New Zealand and Japan, as examples.)

Country calls for activity; it needs rousing engagement more than it needs settlement. I should have comprehended this long ago. After all, having fled the baking suburbs of Brisbane, I have lived most of my adult life in Sydney, in love with the tidal reaches and deepwater bays, thrilled by the sinuous flows of walking tracks and roads that are obliged into divagation because of the bluffs and scribbled shorelines in the flooded canyon that shapes the harbour that laves the glittering city. Landlocked Sydney is *not*. Nor is it governed much by grids. Rather, the place is drawn and maintained by its fluid rhythms. The city lolls not only with the harbour's pulses but also in concert with washes of sunshine and restless breezes, showers and thunderstorms that queue to baste the sandstone ridgelines. There is a quality here, part natural part cultural, that is aqueous.

The art that arises under these conditions needs a particular kind of witnessing; it needs an aesthetic analysis that investigates how creativity proceeds in a world that is suffused with fluidity. This is an aesthetic approach that is interested in formative forces, emergence and adaptation rather than in surveying an inventory of well-wrought *objets d'art*. It is the kind of aesthetic analysis – associative and multi-modal – that is practised by scholars such as Robert Farris Thompson, whose great study *TANGO: the art history of love* is the exemplar. In Thompson's genre of art analysis, the scholar looks to understand how aesthetic forms and cultural practices can mutate to span many media and mutate through generations of cultural producers who are practically connected across space and time. Thompson surfs and serves the multifarious culture of tango, detailing its restlessness but also its consistencies. Understanding tango as a response to Afro-European social intricacies as well as to environmental peculiarities prevailing in South America, he tracks the historical alterations – generation after generation, virtuoso after virtuoso – in the many modes of song, dance, couture and *brio* that comprise tango culture. Indeed, to do this work well, the writer became a dancer and a singer. (The internet is his showcase!) Thompson's version of aesthetic analysis is founded on a determination to tune into the animus of a culture, to know intimately and immersively the motive ingenuities that make tango cohere even as it always shifts and mutates, generation to generation, country to country. This is the kind of aesthetic analysis too – process-attentive rather than product-fixated – that is most pertinent here in our aqueous world.[3]

I have come to this view – setting myself loose from old grounded convictions – after experiencing four special encounters that have worked on me as slow-burn epiphanies. They are revelations that itched first as hunches and then took years to clarify. Three of them derive from New Zealand and one from Sydney. At pertinent moments throughout this essay, to cinch my argument, I will describe each of these little enlightenments.

### First NZ Epiphany

My initial aqueous insight – a New Zealand one – might seem banal on first telling. It is not academic. I was on a plane from Sydney to Auckland, sometime in the late 1990s. Sitting next to me was a fifteen year-old youth who was also travelling alone. We exchanged just four or five minutes of chit chat before he silently bowed to the inevitable – that I had nothing worth talking about – and went under the headphones.

Wherever he is now, I doubt he will remember the conversation we had. I had no lesson for him. But for me, it was different: he changed my mind. The chat went like this. I asked if he was going home. Nah, he said, not really. Some desultory banter revealed that he had been living with relatives in Sydney's western suburbs for a few years. Now he was going to Auckland for a while. Same deal: two or three years, maybe, with other members of his extended family. Then he would probably go back to the Cook Islands for a while, the place of his birth. Or he might end up somewhere else, with other cousins or an aunt and uncle. Maybe LA. Indulging a twinge of concern that was part middle-class and part grounded-Australian, I ventured that it must be tough, not being attached to any one place. Genuinely, courteously, he didn't get what I was talking about. I tried asking the question another way. 'Nah,' he shrugged at last, 'It's what we do. We move around. Always have. It's good.' End of conversation.

I spent the remainder of the flight thinking about this, disturbed at how normalising and laden with thoughtless inertia my insistence on 'placement' had been. I figured 'we' was probably his family. ('It's what we do. We move around.') But maybe 'we' was contemporary Rarotongans. Or Pacific Islanders, acclaimed more generally. I thought about the anthropologist Joel Bonnemaison's evocative account of how some Pacific Islanders identify themselves as, simultaneously, 'trees' and 'canoes'. In other words, Bonnemaison contends, these Islanders know that they come from some place, that they started with roots and with debts and obligations to the ground; but they know too that they quickly and rightly get fashioned early by other aspects of their natural environments as well as by culture, opportunity, family and clan relations. The end result is they become a mobile social entity responsive to forces – natural and cultural – that urge collaboration and ceaseless travel. So each person is always part tree and part canoe.[4] Drawn from a philosophical matrix that is worlds away in space and time from the pre-Socratic Greeks, Bonnemaison's dyad of selfhood helps us see how – in ways uncannily similar to the world construed by the Greeks – water might support all existence. A tree grows on the doused land so that it can become a canoe that overcomes but is also supported by the shifting, encircling ocean.

As I thought about all this in the Auckland-bound airliner, I knew it would have been just creepy of me to nudge my dozing neighbor, to ask him more questions. I wanted to, but I resisted the urge. After all, a plane is like a canoe insofar as you have responsibilities to your fellow-travellers. I let the lad zoom unperturbed into the next draught of his life's voyage.

My point is: to be engaged peripatetically with a scatter of options and obligations distributed round the Pacific is demonstrably a cogent, good way of being in the world, a way supported by systems of expectation and productivity, supported by patterns of social history as well as by tendencies in nature. Your culture might derive as much from a restless system of flows, I realised, as from a permanent foundation in a place.

I thought then about one of my favourite images: the island chart that Tupaia – the Tahitian master navigator who voyaged with James Cook in 1769–70 – had sketched when he was travelling westerly on the *Endeavour*.

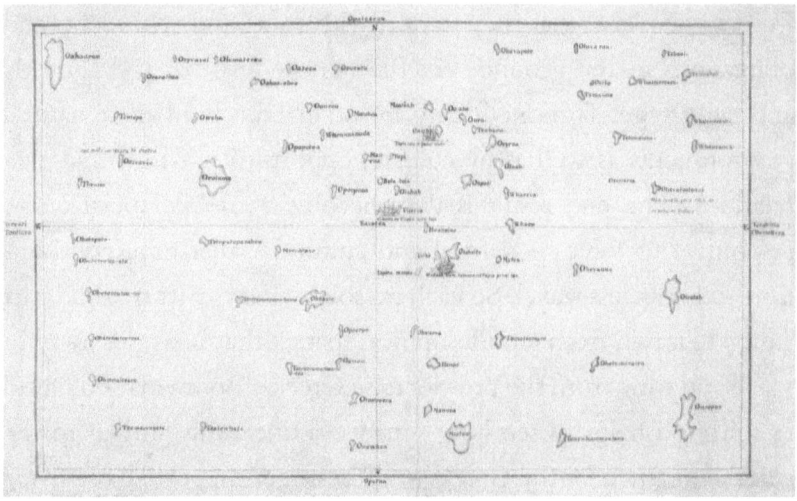

The sense you get when pondering the chart is that it was designed to convey how the islands all float with a kind of tensile gravity that shifts as you, the navigator, shift within the array that is depicted. Rather than being fixed permanently to the earth's surface, the islands are adrift and arrayed in relation to your trajectory. And rather than hovering outside the chart, you the observer are implicated in it, encouraged by the design to get folded into the floating splay of islands. As a reader of the chart, absorbing valency from where you have come from and where you are trying to get to, you perceive certain islands to be immediately present and pressing; others are less pertinent to your immediate predicament and thus all shrink and loiter in the background, as if waiting for the time when a reconfigured cluster of them will get hauled in a cognitive seine toward you, waiting to be made resonant by your need when the trajectory of the voyage requires them to freshen with new charge. The map is just a freeze-frame in a restless flowchart. In your imagination you see the entire durational, jostling and re-configurative slosh of Polynesian navigation.

While the plane kept thrumming east across the Tasman Sea, I looked down and thought about Will Kyselka's great book, *An Ocean in Mind*, where he describes the principles of indigenous Pacific navigation:

> The wayfinder ... knows where he starts and where he wants to go. Along the way he maintains continuous orientation by reading nature's signs and attending to speed and direction. If a storm comes up and the wayfinder loses direction, he's lost. Really lost. After the storm he re-orients as best he can and proceeds on the way.
>
> ... [A wayfinder] reports where he thinks the canoe to be relative to his reference course. The sum of the data gives us a region. Sometimes a large one and sometimes small – a region of the ocean, not a point, where he knows the canoe to be. We take all these bits of data and, picking a most probable point, connect points of probability into a line we call the canoe's presumed course.[5]

Not much is 'solid state' here. Kyselka's book is a cultural history of flux. He explains how navigators make themselves available to all the surrounding forces, steeping themselves in the wafting smells, the shifts in radiance, the surging currents, the phosphorescence, the convoluted behaviour of bird flocks, wind directions and wave shapes, until the ocean's directive impulses begin to transmit in a way that is holistically apparent, moment by moment. Kyselka contrasts these traditional methods of orientation with the systems that were used on the high-tech motorboat that brought him to the outlying island where he boarded the canoe on which his traditional education could commence. Radically different types of navigation are practised on the two different types of vessel, he explains. On the motorboat, the navigators use instruments and previously-published maps for gathering and processing data; whereas on the canoe, only the mind and the senses are deployed in evanescent realtime. On the motorboat, the consciousness is 'external'; but on the canoe, your engagement with the ocean is mindful and 'internal' because you strive to understand how the vectors of yourself and the ocean are indivisible even as you try to determine your own distinct trajectory; on the canoe, you do not imagine yourself outside the scene, as if you could float above it and see a permanent template in it; rather you are within and part of its integrated cohesion such that if you move, all the elements of that contingent coherence must adjust with and through you. On the motorboat, by contrast, technicians spread 'a net over the earth and locate position relative to the intersection of imaginary lines that we call latitude and longitude'; on the canoe, the navigator is 'at the centre of sea and sky, with islands moving along that circle's edge'.[6] The canoe navigator is inside an emerging event, while the motorboat navigator looks down, from the outside, on a chart that is pre-formed, settled and and published to posterity. In a simple but profound summation, Kyselka then explains that it is 'a personal act' to navigate a canoe through the intimately learned ocean.[7]

Up in the plane, I thought about how the traditional method of wayfinding is like the 'flow experience' that governs the creative processes analysed by the psychologist Mihaly Csikszentmihalyi in his influential cognitive-science accounts of creativity. Flow is a sense of engulfing concentration, Csikszentmihalyi maintains, that can overtake anyone who is responsively immersed in the ever-unfolding challenges of a complex situation. Flow can occur when focused attentiveness, peripheral awareness and memory all support improvisation in a continuous routine of problem-solving. Artists experience flow, as do sportspeople and navigators, 'when goals are clear, when above-average challenges are matched to skills, and when accurate feedback is forthcoming'. For someone involved in the flow of a dynamic circumstance, 'concentration focusses on what needs to be done' in such a way that 'irrelevant thoughts, worries, distractions no longer have a chance to appear in consciousness'.[8] Likewise, when attending to the seemingly chaotic impulses in the environment, an immersed navigator finds a way (a 'personal act') through a set of apparently disconnected impedances and affordances. The process of problem-solving aligns actions with reactions through experimentation. No matter how quick and changeful the system might be, the peculiar coherence of the complex circumstance can gradually become evident and available to the absorbed improviser. Csikszentmihalyi identifies at least eight conditions that can combine to produce the experience of flow. These conditions can be summarised as follows:

> First, the experience usually occurs when we confront tasks we have a chance of completing.

> Second, we must be able to concentrate on what we are doing.

Third and fourth, the concentration is usually possible because the task undertaken has clear goals and provides immediate feedback.

Fifth, one acts with a deep but effortless involvement that removes from awareness the worries and frustrations of everyday life.

Sixth, enjoyable experiences allow people to exercise a sense of control over their actions.

Seventh, concern for the self disappears, yet paradoxically the sense of self emerges stronger after the flow experience is over.

Finally, the sense of the duration of time is altered; hours pass by in minutes, and minutes can stretch out to seem like hours.

The combination of all these elements causes a sense of deep enjoyment that is so rewarding people feel that expending a great deal of energy is worthwhile to be able to feel it.[9]

This sounds remarkably similar to the processes of a successful navigator, as reported to Kyselka by an apprentice: 'You've got to concentrate to be a good navigator. You've got to be tense'. The apprentice pauses to consider this assertion and after reflecting for a moment more he balances it with, 'But you've got to relax.' Not satisfied yet, he replaces 'tense' with 'intense', explaining 'because if I'm tense I get tired real fast'.[10]

Tension. Relaxation. As the plane descended into Auckland we were jolted by severe turbulence. Tersely, the pilot came on the intercom and commanded, rather than requested, that we all secure our seatbelts against the coming five minutes. The plane swooped and yawed as we buffeted ever-closer into the ground. The engines howled in exertion and the wind-rudders flapped alarmingly as a gale smacked us around. Then the plane bounced, really hard, on and back off the tarmac and then plopped down again, skidded, gripped, then veered and finally slid to a stop. The intercom came back on, the pilot's voice now smiling with sparkled banter: 'Well, Ladies and Gentlemen, that's another one we can walk away from. Welcome to Auckland, where the time is …' The Rarotongan kid looked across to me, chuckled and raised one eyebrow before blowing out a big long breath.

### Australian Epiphany

I wonder if the immersion in flowing consciousness was ever experienced by the Australian Aboriginal adventurer Gnung-a Gnung-a, who would almost certainly have worked alongside Polynesian mates when he shipped as a crewman aboard the British storeship the *Daedalus* when it voyaged from Sydney Cove through Hawaii to Nootka Sound and back again in 1792. The Sydney Aborigine (known in their language as 'Eora') were probably more receptive to the Islander notions than we might expect. It was well known amongst English sailors that James Cook had received advice from Tupaia throughout a significant portion of the *Endeavour* voyage in 1769 and 1770. Perhaps, as Eora like Gnung-a Gnung-a began to conscript for ocean voyages twenty years later, some seasoned old shipmates still told tales of Tupaia. Perhaps the Eora sensed how similar the ocean navigation was to being in country.

The first place the word 'Eora' was written is probably in the notebooks compiled by William Dawes, a marine lieutenant in the colonising militia that landed at Sydney Cove in January 1788. He brings my second slow-burn epiphany. Over a four-year period Dawes engaged intensively and extensively with Australian Aboriginal culture. He became friends with at least twenty Eora, recording significant swathes of the language spoken around the harbour, observing and growing to respect the spiritual practices and social ceremonies of the locals. In his roles as the chief engineer, astronomer, surveyor and cartographer for the colony, he took long treks into country, sometimes with Eora companions. Chartless in the first instances, these treks were necessarily way-finding exercises. In other words, the forays into country were aqueous kinds of exercises.

What Dawes learned with the Eora was more fluid than solid-state, therefore. But he knew both modes, of course, for he was a marine, under orders to work on sea and land. Moreover he was the astronomer for the colony too, charged with mapping the shifting alignments and guiding constellations adrift in the southern sky. Being out in country with the Eora, even if it was just a short twilight trek to a favourite bathing beach, must have felt like the undulating opposite to his surveyor's land-locking vocation. For the Eora would have demonstrated to him how to be ceremonially immersed and narratively implicated in the country, which included the wheeling sky above and the shimmering harbor which the locals criss-crossed sprightly in canoes. With the Eora, the country was not objectively distanced, not externally oriented to fixed reference-points that had been mapped from an ideal point somewhere above their terrain. For the Eora, space and time seemed to combine moment by moment in the peoples' consciousness, right there and then in a fluid, instantaneous insinuation of every perceptible and imaginable detail. Country was a communal and unfolding event, a contingency always in process rather than a product captured, published and conserved in cadastral registrations.

Deborah Bird Rose is compelling on this topic. To be in country most beneficially, she explains, you have to be absorbed by it; you have to redistribute yourself in it and be directed and determined by its dynamics. It is a process strikingly similar to traditional Pacific navigation, so much of it being about connectivity and flow:

> A 'healthy' or 'good' country is one in which all the elements do their work.
>
> They all nourish each other because there is no site, no position, from which the interest of one cannot be disengaged from the interests of others in the long term. Self-interest and the interest of all of the other living components of country (the self-interest of kangaroos, barramundi, eels and so on) cannot exist independently of each other.[11]

I have concentrated on these topics, arcane as they might seem at first, because my epiphanies have shown how all human activity, especially art, can be deeply and distinctively affected by the ways Indigenous country and the impulses of the ocean all instruct us in changefulness. In the Southern part of the world, where I live and work, there is presently an aqueous quality that pushes out of the Pacific and into modern experience, including into 'Western' art. This aqueous quality has given rise to an aesthetic that is pressing and impressive now because the concerns that ocean-informed improvisers and artists have always addressed are currently concerns that are surging into the everyday experience of most inheritors of the Cartesian tradition worldwide. This preoccupation with flow and changefulness is something even more profound than the revolution of perception and conception that Bernard Smith detailed so famously in *European Vision and the South Pacific*.[12] For with the aqueous sensibility, it is not just that objects are seen in new ways; rather, the acceptance of object-ness itself – the purportedly permanent status of things – can dissolve in the fluid zones of the South. Objects lose definition. And *events* become paramount.

In the present moment of global history, with planetary travel and worldwide networks of instantaneous communication now normal, all human experience is interfused and in motion. Aqueous qualities define everyday existence in markets, in mines, in parliaments and places that might at first seem entirely unrelated to the coastlines of Auckland, Sydney or the Pacific Islands.

Marine officer Dawes has helped me grasp this enigma. I have been guided also by modern scholars like Greg Dening, Geoff Park and Anne Salmond, who have enriched our understanding of how the European sensibility – that had been fostered by the Western Enlightenment – was thrown into philosophical and psychological tumult when northern-hemisphere voyagers came to the South Pacific late in the eighteenth century.[13] Invariant and mechanistic worldviews bolstered by notions such as 'the great chain of being' and nominalism (I will write more about this momentarily), were loosened by Islanders' and Aborigines' modes of navigating with and through the world of constantly contingent relationships.[14] As Dening put it so pithily, many Europeans found themselves 'relativised by new political experiences … and new cultural experiences of otherness'[15] in the Pacific, in the realm that Herman Melville called 'the watery part of the world'.[16] Through many centuries these water-borne experiences have always given rise to art. Distinctive art. And such 'aqueous' art – undeniably part of global culture now – has histories currently unfolding that are distinctly different from the standard European/American ones.

Such 'otherness' (so-called from the Enlightenment-trained, European viewpoint), influenced how the status of objects, including *objets d'art*, might be understood afresh in aqueous experiences. William Dawes grasped this two centuries ago. He noticed how the world and the language and the speakers and listeners he was studying with the Eora were in constant flux, defined mainly by ever-shifting relationships amongst themselves.

The classicist Anne Carson sees this kind of changefulness as especially active in the way language works for cultures that have and need little or no writing. We who have inherited the Enlightenment protocols of reason, critical distance and staunch perspective know that to write is to manage words as things (and things as words). We know too that to set words in place on the page is to have a *status* that expedites the analysis, evaluation and hierarchisation of the things they represent. In an oral culture, however, where one speaks into the fleeting air, a different world is implied or arranged. Carson elaborates. In a world evoked by unwritten languages, subjects and objects tend not to be rigidly fixed. The boundaries between the self and the other (be it human, animal, vegetable or mineral) blur more readily:

> Complete openness to the environment is a condition of optimum awareness and alertness for [a person operating in an oral culture, such that] … a continual fluent interchange of sensual impressions and responses between the environment and himself is the proper condition of

his physical and mental life. To close his senses off from the outside world would be counterproductive to life and to thought.[17]

Carson is referring explicitly to the transition from oral to written modes as she has studied it within ancient Greek culture. But her ideas help us think about what must have been felt when Dawes brought the written mode of language to the Sydney people:

> Reading and writing require focusing the mental attention upon a text by means of the visual sense. As an individual reads and writes he gradually learns to close or inhibit the input of his senses, to inhibit or control the responses of his body, so as to train energy and thought upon the written words. He resists the environment outside him by distinguishing and controlling the one inside him. … In making the effort he becomes aware of the interior self as an entity separable from the environment and its input, controllable by his own mental action … the individual personality gathers itself to resist disintegration.[18]

With writing, words are no longer an airy event comprised just of uttered breath pulsing in a transient, commingled world of overlapped sound. Writing makes a technologised scene where words are clipped things fixed long and visibly on a page (comparable to the charts that Kyselka studied on the motorboat). Carson focuses her argument by concentrating on edges and frames:

> [Once they are imprinted on a surface] … words have edges. Heard words may have no edges, or varying

edges; oral traditions may have no concept of 'word' as a fixed and bounded vocable. Homer's word for 'word' (epos) includes the meanings 'speech,' 'tale,' 'song,' 'line of verse,' or 'epic poetry as a whole.' All are breathable, the edges are irrelevant.[19]

Thus Dawes brought edged words to lock the world into objective status with his records and measurements? Yes. But paradoxically no. For he was also an innovator. He was in the avant garde of early-Romantic science, part of a generation of questers who sensed fluidity all around them. As Richard Holmes explains, these scientists worked '[in] reaction against the idea of a purely mechanistic universe, the mathematical world of Newtonian physics, the hard material world of objects and impacts'; instead they 'favoured a softer "dynamic" science of invisible powers and mysterious energies, of fluidity and transformations, of growth and organic change'.[20] For example, there was Dawes' work as an astronomer. Through his framing devices he tracked how the stars were actually uncontainable – in the long run *unframe-able* therefore – how they were moving in three dimensions and in a concussion of different rhythms inside deep space and time. Also, he was a weather-monitor, noting five times a day the varying vectors and pressures in the air, comprehending over four annual cycles how the animating breath of the southern world could *not* be readily methodised.[21] And he was a marine, a man trained to know slipperiness and indeterminacy, trained not to rely on solidity, trained to move back and forth between contradictory states and contrasting environments. Furthermore, with his work on the page, he often reneged and redrafted. He used the pencil (with all the transience it afforded) as much as he used the permanence of the inked pen. Frequently in his notebooks, he sketched and erased, underscored and overscored in penciled 'rough hand'. He set down the edged words, but he blurred and shifted them too.

To say this another way, Dawes was loath to endorse the nominalist account of worldly experience, the kind of account that Dr Samuel Johnson – the consummate word-fixer, lister and edge-cutter – had affirmed so famously when he refuted relativistic thinking by kicking a roadside stone and declaring it the basis of his worldview.[22] With a pragmatic, Newtonian and therefore utterly British construal of existence, nouns stuck labels on objects. In this written version of reality, 'nouned' objects wait, stolidly composed, for sovereign speakers to exert influence on them, to exploit them with verbs and to deploy adjectives in nuanced recalibration of their given qualities.

By contrast Dawes found reality could swirl like water when he was with the Eora. The most telling moment in his notebooks comes when he records how there were different grammatical constructions for Eora speaking in the first-person-plural, depending on whether the speaker was referring to 'we two' or to 'we all'. It seemed that a speaker was always more attentive to the *communal* voice rather than the personal. And the laws were vehement, demanding that the speaker invoke the collectivity in exactly the right way. To emphasise this point, at one stage the Aborigine known as Patyegarang – Dawes' principle informer on the workings of the language – took pains to change the already-written record of the grammar in her speech, when she realised that she had not taken account of someone extra (a young girl named Pundul) who had been in the ambit of an earlier conversation. This is perhaps the major epiphany in the Dawes notebooks.

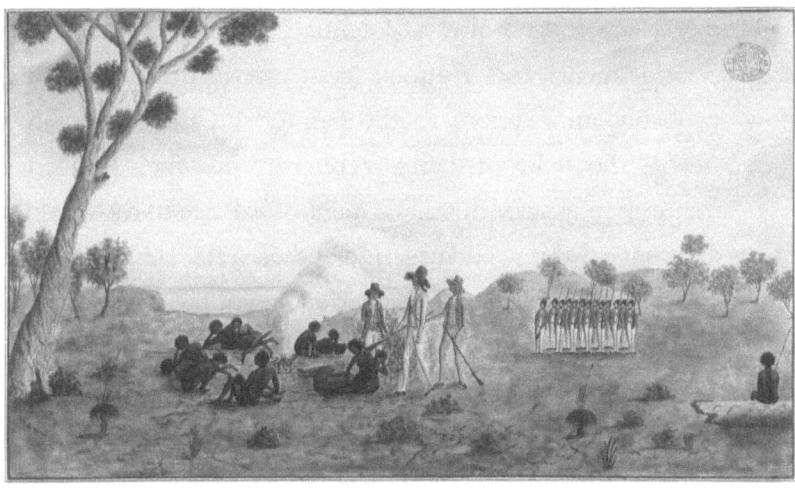

*The Port Jackson Painter, 'Mr White, Harris and Laing with a Party of Soldiers visiting Botany Bay Colebee at that place, when wounded', 1791(?), Natural History Museum, London.*

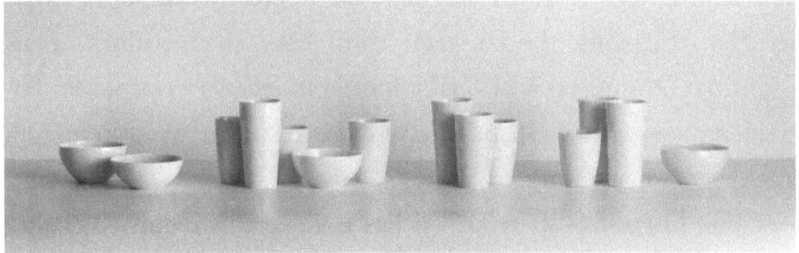

*Gwyn Hanssen Pigott, 'Kinder Trail'. Image courtesy of the Victoria & Albert Museum.*

Noting Patyegarang's attentiveness to collectivity reminds me of a remarkable lecture that I attended in 1995 at the Museum of Sydney, where the Aboriginal Elder Gerry Bostock interpreted several First Fleet paintings by concentrating on the spatial and postural arrangements in groups of Indigenous figures portrayed in the scenes. Understanding how subjectivity can operate in a collective and integrative manner, one senses mutual responsibility as a force at work amongst all objects and subjects in space and time, so much so that the entities an Englishman might want to call 'objects' are indeed always potentially changing to become 'subjects' and 'agents' too. Bostock spent careful time explaining how (probably unbeknown to the painter) at least one of the group-scenes showed a medicinal ceremony in which Indigenes were attending to exactly this adjustment of balance in the worldly forces that move through and organise bodies, trees, landmarks and all the other elements that make up a tract of country. Configured this way, it is the valency suffusing and atomising things that forms the world; a scene is always ready to alter, to recalibrate and to have its basic entities transmogrify, depending on how the elements are assembled, relative to one another, in any specific place, under the influence of possibility vying with predetermination, at any particular moment.

So it is, too, with the language that represents the Eora world to all participants: the language must have changefulness in its grammar, it must be relationally motile in its every operation. For the language actively shapes the world even as the words represent whatever is happening.

The linguist Robert Dixon has noticed this recursive characteristic in most Aboriginal languages in Australia. Because words are made of breath, and because breath is spirit which is the power that agitates the world, then it follows necessarily that native speakers take great care with utterance, using generic terms so that their specific meanings within a particular statement have to be apprehended in the protective context of knowledge shared and agreed among the speaker and the addressees. For example, a word that, on first hearing, might seem to mean 'knee' can also mean many other instances of conjunction, suppleness or turning, depending on the surrounding verbal system in which it is being deployed. With the Indigenous languages, every assertion tends to be specifically contextual, which is to say exactly environmental and obliged to everything else evoked in the statement. Every utterance is dramaturgically managed for distributing the world's energy in a safe and manageable way. Every utterance is always colluding with the world as a forceful event rather than accounting for the world as a composite set of given objects or resources that are merely represented by the language. Aboriginal words tend away from being nominalist, therefore; they tend not to imply a rigid concordance to some locked-off or pre-formed order. Instead words are treated in a more energetic and gaseous manner, especially in the way they take their shape, weight and valency from everything else around them. This is because the world transmogrifies like that too, having at least as much spirit in it as matter. The world does not have much status; it has dynamics. The world alters from moment to moment, from utterance to utterance, from relational configuration to configuration.

In his bravura essay 'Nominalist and Realist', written for a markedly different context, Ralph Waldo Emerson said it with riddles, but in a way that is germane to the mutability that Dixon has described and that Dawes experienced:

> Really, all things and persons are related to us, but according to our nature they act on us not at once but in succession, and we are made aware of their presence one at a time. All persons, all things which we have known, are here present, and many more than we see; the world is full. … No sentence will hold the whole truth, and the only way in which we can be just, is by giving ourselves the lie; Speech is better than silence; silence is better than speech; — All things are in contact; every atom has a sphere of repulsion; — Things are, and are not, at the same time.

# Changescapes

All things are in contact! Generally speaking, in Aboriginal languages there is a heightened awareness of the potential for realignment and interfusion in any set of elements, in any prevailing condition. Typically, as wood might burn to be fire and an animal is ready to become meat, so an utterance referring to wood must have the potential to connote fire; the same for animal and meat; and so on. Things are and are not. With this dramatisation of potentiality, every speakable thing and action must be understood not as something pre-formed that gets merely qualified or modified by minor adjustments from outside its solid constitution. Rather, every portion of the world is inseparable from every other portion and must be construed as part of a set of changeful possibilities, all interdependent and constantly determined by the relationships that host it. Wood can be fire. Rain can be blood. An animal can be killed and in its death it can become life when it changes to meat for a man.

All things are in contact while they are potentially becoming something else. Seeping into each other. Insinuating and motivating.

It works like this with aqueous aesthetics too. There is something artful in the way relational components in fluid scenes are constantly altering. For let's not forget that 'art' is the word that connotes transformation. This is why we have words like 'articulate' and 'arthritis': art occurs in the joint, the place in space or time where a turn occurs. And aesthetics addressing such dynamics must offer accounts of processes detailing constant alteration and adjustment rather than auditing finished products. Thus, aqueous conditions must give rise to an aesthetics of changefulness. An aesthetics devoted to describing, evaluating, analyzing and understanding artistic outputs as changescapes.

## Aqueous Aesthetics

From an Australian perspective, such aesthetics would guide us into a more telling appreciation of works like the Port Jackson Painter's rendition of the spatial configurations in the English militia and Aborigines at Botany Bay (see illustration). Practising such aesthetics, we would examine the valencies – the attractions and repulsions, the generative incompletions and implied movements – that are strung amongst all the components in the scene. We would look not only for a naturalistic snapshot of horticulture or for portraits of personal comportment; rather we would work our way into the picture and begin to sense the impulses within in it, how they are organising the represented world. We would think about how space and time are being constructed by nature and culture in constant contention, how each represented moment is myriad different processes articulating with us and with each other, and how the observer cannot sensibly be separated from the forces that are making every scene, moment by moment. We might begin to understand the painting not as an object but as a conduit to entangled, world-creating forces that require divination and precise, endless new calibrations. All that is solid might then defer to the impulsions in the air and to the time scales that swirl all around every present moment.

To bring the focus into more recent times: such aqueous aesthetics would help us acknowledge and investigate the force at play and always altering in the diffused, shadowy light that steams amongst the objects in a Gwyn Hanssen Pigot assemblage (see illustration). We might see how the power in the configuration stems from the ensemble and the relationships available within it; from the fuzzed visible edges of the vessels, from the indistinction between figure and ground, from the difficulty in discriminating positive and negative space, rather than from each exquisite and solid, singular object. We might see all the relational flux inside the system and know that it makes Pigot's 'still-life' arrays so paradoxically active, shifty, invigorating and endlessly eventful.

To ponder these issues more deeply, let's wonder how might aqueous aesthetics grant us a better understanding of complexity when it is rendered in the form of edgeless acoustic art? Consider for example the compositional symphonics generated in the improvised music of the three-piece band The Necks. In the band's real-time compositions, we can hear a wholistic intelligence cohering processually when the pianist, drummer and bassist each negotiate the deceptively simple riffs of repetition and adjustment that the musicians interweave as they create their hour-long sound-events.[23] We grasp how each performance is a changescape, an experiment to measure and activate the reverberant, acoustic liveliness of whatever venue is hosting each particular performance. We find ways to analyse the cohering momentum that gels (but also melts) amongst the three performers as they provoke and react to each other whilst also attending to the delicate integrity of the composition as it emerges eventfully from its seemingly simple but restless componentry.

### Second NZ Epiphany

Scanning further for other projects that demand and reward aqueous aesthetics, I think of *Mana Waka* (1938–1990), which was brought to light by Merata Mita in collaboration with activists, craftspeople and artists working across cultures and across several generations. I first encountered the project at an academic conference in Melbourne in 1992. It is not nearly as famous as it ought to be. Some people will know it as a film, but it is more than a single object, given how it is the activation of social, aesthetic and spiritual principles that show how humanity in the Pacific has thrived through the centuries. A longrunning process rather than just a finished cinematic product, it is an endless series of negotiations, actions and reactions, co-operations and dispersions of self-interest that show how all things in the natural and social worlds need to flow and be connected. Its force presses forwards and backwards in time.

*Mana Waka* started in the 1930s in New Zealand when the eminent Waikato leader Te Kirihaehae Te Puea Herangi resolved to perpetuate canoe-building skills in her community. This meant not only fostering the great craft skills required to cull the enormous vessels from the giant trees in the ancient forests; it also meant reviving ecological knowledge as well as rituals of communal cohesion and distributed obligation that traditionally caused every canoe to be a psychological, social and spiritual configuration, the construction of which integrated community memory, ambition, design intelligence and technical know-how all aligned to the dynamics of natural processes and resources. Under the executive supervision of the revered Elder Ranui Maupakanga, the carver Piri Poutapu supervised the refurbishment of a beloved old canoe, Te Winika, thereby training a new generation of young carvers. Additionally, several years of lobbying and fund raising by Te Puea led to the construction of a great new canoe, named Ng-toki-mata-whao-rua. During its construction and possibly also throughout the refurbishment of Te Winika, the photographer R.G.H. Manley was permitted to document the process cinematographically. No sound was recorded but the movie footage that survives (and that lay unprocessed and uninspected for fifty years) is a luminous treasure subject to sacred Maori sanctions.

In 1983 the New Zealand Film Archive was authorized (by Te Arikinui Dame Te Atairangikāhu) to strike prints from the negatives and to consider what greater use could be made of the material. Merata Mita, along with the editor Annie Collins and the Archive Director Jonathan Dennis, retreated to the Turangawaewae Marae to edit the project into a feature-length documentary. But *Mana Waka* is unlike any documentary you have seen before. Through communal consultation but also through delicate attunement to the rhythms of tree-finding and tree-felling, adzing, carving and shaping, a film of the canoe has been made in such a manner that it is like a *film-as-canoe*. Which is to say the film has an intensified symbolic order that is conceptually and formally inseparable from the community that kept the design principles in shared memory, inseparable from the crew of craftspeople, and inseparable from the forest that supplied the tree. Furthermore, fortifying the canoe as it takes shape throughout the film, there is a thrilling, freshly created symphony of a new soundscape composed of forest noises, including the 're-animation' of certain birds that have become extinct and absent from the forests since the 1930s. Causing integration and harmony on many levels, the *Mana Waka* thus interweaves communal remembrances with oratorical and narrative sessions plus dances, song cycles and planning seminars and dispute resolutions that were prompted in the process of fashioning the great craft. Improvisatory, re-animating, recursive, restless, sustaining, aqueous – the project is so much more than just a film.

After viewing and hearing *Mana Waka*, after being immersed in all its elements, you feel re-orchestrated. You sense that your self has been re-distributed across time and space, across different levels of different cultures, across generations, across the forest, into the edit-suite in the Marae, into the intense concentration behind every carving-stroke and hammer-blow that has made the canoe and made the film, into the confabulations and contestations of the community that has brought (and with every screening, continues to bring) the canoe out of their heads and out of the trees, till finally you plunge collectively – with the builders, with the ancestors, with your fellow-spectators and with the canoe – into the mothering ocean.

So *Mana Waka* had commenced before Merata Mita and her collaborators knew of it. During the 1930s the canoe-building project had activated centuries-old practices and allegiances in such a way that (via Manley's film camera) the relationships, skills and specialized knowledge associated with the canoes were stored and made ready to flow into the future, into 1990 and beyond, where the footage is illuminated again after being realigned intricately and devoutly on the edit-bench, just as the canoe itself had been assembled, in all its complexity, at the great carving-pits all those decades earlier. Through the stewardship of Mita and her intergenerational and multi-institutional crew, *Mana Waka* has been brought to light as a memory-system that activates social relations and material dexterities from the past while, like a genealogical chant that honours all things, beasts and people of the forest and the ocean, the film will continue to illuminate and galvanise generation upon generation as culture and nature voyage together into the future.

### Conclusion – Third NZ Epiphany

On one of my trips to Wellington, maybe fifteen years ago, I spent a day with Geoff Park, author of *Nga Uruora: the Groves of Life*, which is one of the great scholarly works to have come from our watery part of the world. Setting out from the Central Business District, Geoff took me walking along contour lines that were concreted and dry now but that had been shaped centuries earlier by countless creek surges and downpour run-offs leading to wetlands where museums and shopping centres now squat.

Then by car we went up to a headland to see how the vegetation still held mottled memories of a vestigial landform shaped by water, wind and brackish reed meadows that had been dried and covered over now with modern engineering but that were clearly still flowing through and around the recently installed solidness. We then motored down into the north side of town, where we left the car and set out on foot again, this time to trace a watercourse that was refusing the cemented drainage regulations imposed by dutiful Councils. Along this ancient flow-line, the water itself was often not evident but particular plants and birds were on show, witnesses to the proximity of the water, evidence that despite so much recent impedance the aqueous qualities of this harbour town were still pushing into everyday experience, dissolving the tidy barriers that are supposed to be separating past, present and future.

That day with Geoff Park came vividly to mind not long ago, when I was holed up in a public library in drought-stricken Melbourne, borrowing air-conditioned ease on a torrid afternoon, reading Robert Pogue Harrison's provocative study of memorial and funerary practices, *The Dominion of the Dead*. There is a vivid passage early in the book, where Harrison offers his credo:

> Whatever the rift that separates their regimes, nature and culture have at least this much in common: both compel the living to serve the interests of the unborn. Yet they differ in their strategies in one decisive respect: culture perpetuates itself through the power of the dead, while nature, as far as we know, makes no use of this resource except in a strictly organic sense.[24]

There is a sense of endlessness and historical flow that cultures demand of their artists. And if one is to write a history of the artistry that animates cultures, then that art history must be less interested in things or in objects of art than in the actions or flowing creative processes that cause coherence to emerge, through art, within the raw world of space, time and change. This account of flow and mutability is an aqueous aesthetics.

Sitting in the still library, wondering why Harrison's book was resonating so strongly for me, I flicked back through my notebook to find something I had transcribed just days before, from the poet Stephane Mallarme: because 'objects are already in existence, it is not necessary to create them … all we have to do is grasp the relationships among them'.[25]

Guided thus by Mallarme, I recalled yet again that exhilarating day with Geoff Park, when we chased actual flow-lines that were still pushing out from the past, when we saw how those lines continued to countervail the stasis of death, when we sensed how nature and culture could collaborate to keep continuity in space, place, people, matter, memory and time. I thought about the movement of relationships amongst all the factors and vectors comprising history in the aqueous parts of the world. I thought about my slow-burn epiphanies: people understanding themselves as trees-and-canoes and aeroplanes; the relational intelligence of Tupaia; everything that William Dawes began to understand in Eora country; the negotiations and creative remembrances that had been activated in the making and exhibiting of *Mana Waka*. And I began to understand just a little more intimately how there is something dynamic in the southern part of the world, something that needs its dedicated historians so that the necessary flows and creative processes and galvanized relationships can all arc out from this, our South Pacific juncture in space and time, to serve the interests of the entire world that yet remains unborn.

## Notes

1. These pre-Socratic ideas have been given a modern gloss in Joseph Margolis, *The Flux of History and the Flux of Science*, Berkeley: University of California Press, 1993.
2. See Deborah Bird Rose, *Nourishing Terrains: Australian Aboriginal Views of Landscape and Wilderness*, Canberra: Australian Heritage Commission, 1996.
3. This style of 'alternative' art history inspired by Thompson is more like aesthetics; it is different from, but not disparaging of, the more traditional art history that produces impressive and influential projects such as Peter Brunt and Nicholas Thomas's canonical *Art in Oceania*, London: Thames and Hudson, 2012. The aesthetics that I am pursuing is much more closely aligned to the approaches found in projects such as *Liquid State*, the special issue of the journal *Reading Room*, 4 (2010), published by the Auckland Art Gallery, and the major exhibition curated by Ian Wedde at the Rotorua Museum, *He Korowai o te Wai: The Mantle of Water*, Nov 2008 – April 2009.
4. See Joel Bonnemaison, 'The Tree and the Canoe: roots and mobility in Vanuatu societies' in *Pacific Viewpoint*, Vol 26, No 1 (1985), pp. 30–62.
5. Will Kyselka, *An Ocean in Mind*, Honolulu: University of Hawaii Press, 1987, p. 169–71
6. Kyselka, pp. 168–69.
7. Kyselka, p. 206.
8. Mihaly Csikszentmihalyi, 'The Flow Experience and its significance for human psychology', in Mihaly Csikszentmihalyi and Isabella Selega Csikszentmihalyi (eds), *Optimal Experience: psychological studies of flow in consciousness*, Cambridge: Cambridge University Press, 1988, p.34.
9. Mihaly Csikszentmihalyi, *Flow: the psychology of optimal experience*, New York: Harper and Row, 1990, p. 49.
10. Kyselka, pp. 62–3.
11. Rose, *Nourishing Terrains*, p. 10. For another insightful essay on country and fluidity, see Maureen Fuary, 'Reading and riding the waves: the sea as known universe in Torres Strait' in *Historic Environment*, volume 22, number 1 (2009), pp. 32–7.
12. Bernard Smith, *European Vision and the South Pacific 1768–1850: a study in the history of art and ideas*, Oxford: Clarendon Press, 1960.
13. I will refer to specific texts by Dening and Park presently. For Anne Salmond, see: *Between worlds: early exchanges between Maori and Europeans, 1773–1815*, Auckland: Viking, 1997; and *The trial of the cannibal dog: the remarkable story of Captain Cook's encounters in the South Seas*, New Haven: Yale University Press, 2003.

14  See Arthur O. Lovejoy, *The Great Chain of Being: a study in the history of an idea*, Cambridge (Mass.): Harvard University Press, 1936.
15  Greg Dening, *Mr Bligh's Bad Language: passion, power and theatre on the bounty*, Cambridge: Cambridge University Press, 1992, p. 123.
16  Herman Melville, *Moby-Dick: or, The Whale*, New York: Harper and Brothers, 1851, p. 1.
17  Carson, p. 44.
18  Carson, p. 44.
19  Carson, p. 50.
20  Richard Holmes, *The Age of Wonder: how the Romantic generation discovered the beauty and terror of science*, London: Harper Press, 2008, p. xviii.
21  See Robert J. McAfee (ed.), *Dawes' Meteorological Journal*, Canberra: Federal Government Department of Science and Technology, Canberra, 1981. See also Richard Hamblyn, *The Invention of Clouds: how an amateur meteorologist forged the language of the skies*, Picador, London, 2001.
22  James Boswell, *The Life of Samuel Johnson, LLD*, Vol.1, London: J. Davis, 1791, p.218.
23  See and hear the band's website: http://www.thenecks.com/
24  Robert Pogue Harrison, *The Dominion of the Dead*, Chicago: The University of Chicago Press, 2003, p. ix.
25  Seishi Yamaguchi, citing Mallarme, requoted in the 'Introduction' to Seishi's *The Essence of Modern Haiku*, Atlanta: Mangajin, 1993, p.xix.

## 3

## THE RISE OF MULTIMEDIA SYSTEMS

In 1957 Ian Watt published *The Rise of the Novel*. Soon endorsed as a classic of cultural history, the book analysed 'the enduring connexions between the distinctive literary qualities of the novel and those of the society in which it began and flourished'.[1] This society – eighteenth-century western Europe – had become complicated. With the waning of the Church and the discrediting of the notion of the divine rights of kings, most European states were experiencing the rise of mercantilism motivated by the bourgeoisie, an ascendant new class of store-tenders or burghers. 'Common people' began to imagine that they might take charge of their own destiny. All this seemed strange. Unguided. Unprecedented. Novel.

So a story-form was perfected which allowed readers to consider options and anticipate the effects of actions. While imbibing this novel type of text, readers could establish a scene – really felt but not entirely real – where they could pose some orienting questions. For instance:

> If I acted like this, entirely self-motivated, what might flow from the assertion of my new freedoms?

or ...

> How is the old, customary world being renovated by all the new experiences that are so suddenly available?

or …

> Within these settings, what gaggle of testy characters, impulses and belief systems might I encounter as I grant my malleable personality imaginative latitude?

Seeking to understand why this type of text – soon tagged in quick parlance as 'the novel' – emerged suddenly and with so much influence during the early eighteenth century, Watt started from the premise that artistic forms often mimic the psychological, social and political conditions prevalent in the particular era that gives rise to them. He contended that early novelists such as Daniel Defoe and Henry Fielding developed literary techniques for dramatising the emergence of the bourgeois individual, with his or her private sensibility, with his or her responsibility to create self-interested opportunities with the need for self-reflective interior monologues with which to assess the relationship between a persona and the world. Watt showed how writers quickly innovated some textual conventions to sketch settings and evoke the thought-flows and mood-swings of focal characters in imagined narrative worlds which readers could compare to their own, lived worlds. And he showed how these characters might stand in and speak for the readers themselves as citizens tried to grasp the intricacies of an ever-altering life proliferating with new details and secular opportunities. The way they worked on and in the reader, the novelistic characters were experimental and speculative rather than didactic.

Different from the allegory and the religious parable, which are part of the oral tradition and which reinforce established moral codes, the novel arose to facilitate ethical innovation, to help readers scrutinise and speculate about the intellectual and emotional complications of an altering political universe. To this end, the novel was invented as a kind of new technology whereby readers could examine psychic models of a possible personality. Referring to these models and matching them against their received knowledge of lived experience, readers could measure options for themselves. Here was a cultural form that empowered people to reflect on all the novelty that defined their changeful times. No wonder it was suddenly popular. It was needed. It was shaped by and for the contemporary culture. It was pertinent to something urgent.

Watt shows that by examining the structural characteristics of new cultural forms, you can gain insight into phases of psychic, political and philosophical flux. By studying how aesthetic and semantic systems engage with the intellect and the sensorium of the user, you can understand the temper of the times. When a new form of art or a popular mode of communication arises and takes hold, it reflects changes that have recently occurred or are presently occurring in psychology and society. Or to say it bluntly, cultural forms tend to get invented and become popular at exactly the time they are needed. Cultural forms cause change and, a little paradoxically, they also reflect how change has already commenced under the impulsion of forces that are not principally aesthetic.

Contemporary cultural forms show some of the occulted workings of their confusing moment. In this process, there is usually an interplay between intuition and intellection, between speculative proposition about what might be possible and reflective evaluation of what is already operative. This interplay creates discourse, which leads to analytical knowledge, enabling increased efficiency and evocative power in a cultural form as it continues to evolve in consort with the workings of the world.

Through this process, the novel would eventually be superseded (which is not to say eliminated) by a new predominant form of narrative modelling – cinema – which emerged at a time when individual psychologies were changing yet again, this time to absorb the modern world's kinetics (hence the name: cinema). Thus yet another cultural form arose, this time to represent and analyse the tumult of sensory 'attack' that assailed every individual psyche once the speedy, mechanical modes of transport, communication and commodity production became widespread during the industrial revolution. With the machine-age and the urban explosion that industrialisation caused, the modern world was being re-defined by the way energy was expressed urgently within a newly compressed world of rapid, mechanical rhythm. And cinema mimicked this shift in impetus. It was consumed avidly worldwide, right from the outset, because it excited individual psyches with its percussive assemblages of nervous stimuli. Keenly attuned to each viewer's sensory experience within the urban-industrial tumult, cinema was the aesthetic form arising from and mimicking the modern metropolis.

Which means political forces were at play in the rise of cinema. The start of the twentieth century, when cinema loomed all around the world, was a time when new nations and social masses were forming, when throngs were wondering how to fuse several scattered constituencies into new states. Thus in conjunction with other distance-devouring technologies, especially the railroad and the telegraph, cinema helped individuals and communities imagine unified new worlds gathered in a spatio-temporal frame where previously there had been only estranged and disconnected populations clustered in locations that had been unable to synchronise across great administrative time lags. With the advent of cinema, audiences could envisage associations with far-flung people and places all meshing in 'organic' rhythms as fast as heartbeats and almost as quick as thought. The movies projected lively protagonists in a welter of social scenarios. Thus with the aid of cinema a new nation – a new social, spatio-temporal amalgam – could be envisaged where once it had been unimaginable.

How so? Film editors deployed the principle of montage to federate new states of possibility. For the crowds assembled in the smoky theatres, seeing these new states could lead to believing. This happened in Japan, France, Britain, USA and Australia, to name just the obvious cases. (It was the official reason for the establishment of John Grierson's legendary documentary unit in Britain during the 1920s: the unit was instructed to show the nation to the nation.)

Consider Australia circa 1901, at the inauguration of the Federal Government: cinema enabled people in Gympie, Sydney and Adelaide, let's say, to share a perceptual and a conceptual frame where they had previously been dissociated. An associative imagination was fostered. Civic reality and cinematic possibility: each reflected and impelled the other. A nation could be construed as a new federation, and this new order could be imagined in place of the squabbling states that had previously been misaligned in geographical and ideological alienation.

But cinema has its limits. Understanding this, we can start contemplating the rise of digital multimedia systems in our own era. A definitive characteristic of the movies is the way they 'lock off' their several dynamic parts into a final version: the 'release print'. This ultimate inflexibility of cinema is similar to the way most national-scale communities responded to the turbulence of modernity by insisting that their societies first innovate and then synchronise energetically to the machine world before stabilising permanently once the new political state was realised. As its production regimens drive toward 'lock off', cinema is a conservative form, like nationalism. Cinema and nationalism: each serves a popular, paradoxical desire for the acknowledgement and the cessation of change. Indeed, this is one of the traits we love about cinema: it shows us the thrill of energetic convergence and world-creation at the same time as it proposes an eventual end to flux and uncertainty. With a film, the final edit is a stable state, a kingdom of kinetic excitement with a reassuring climate of completion.

Comparing the kinship of cinema and nationalism with the contemporary dyad of digital media and transnationalism (or globalisation), it is clear that digital multimedia systems have arisen to reflect and impel our contemporary psychic and social conditions. Like cinema, digital multimedia can federate disparate elements (sounds, texts, graphics, perspectives, vistas and audio-visual rhythms) into astonishing new configurations. These similarities prompted Lev Manovich, in his influential *The Language of New Media*, to create a myth about multimedia being first generated literally out of cinematic material, out of old film stock stippled with data-entry punctures in Konrad Zuse's 'digital computer' constructed in 1936.[2] But unlike cinema (and unlike nationalism), digital multimedia produces syntheses that are always explicitly provisional. (Yes, in this respect it is like transnationalism.) Because of the dynamics of its file structures and the integrating, evolving codes that get applied to those files, any digital multimedia configuration is a contentious event in a continuous process rather than a completed, content-full object; it is always ready to be dismantled and re-assembled into new alignments as soon as the constituent files retreat to their databases after having been contingently federated in response to momentarily prevailing 'world conditions'.

In other words, because multimedia rarely gets 'locked-off', its component elements can always be pulled apart, sent back to their repositories, enhanced with fresh qualities and metadata, and then instantaneously re-arranged into newly iterated federations. (Yes, in this respect it is like our unstable contemporary lives, so buffeted with ever-altering values, opportunities, anxieties, histories and obligations all upwelling because of globalised commerce and communication, migration and multi-culturalism.) By dramatising divergence and dispersion as well as convergence, a digital multimedia system can react to variant stimuli from the environment or from its investigative participants (who are part of the environment, actually). A digital multimedia system can re-conform itself restlessly in ways that a cinema print is not designed to do. Such a system can reflect and impel our lives of relational engagement within a myriad influences networked in ways that have altered our attitudes to the local, the remote, the immediate, the reverberant.

One challenge when writing about these protean new forms is that, on the page, it is difficult to bring in the concrete evidence. When writing about writing, one can quote an exemplary section of text and analyse it *in text*. By contrast, with a digital multimedia system, the commentator must evoke the exemplar verbally, in the alien medium of fixed text, before using those stolid words to analyse the system's non-verbal potency and shiftiness. Similar 'ekphrastic' issues confront the cinema or the music critic, of course. But at least cinema and music now have lexicons of tropes and canons of 'classics' which can be nominated so readers and

## The Rise of Multimedia Systems

writers all know somewhat the thing they have gathered around. Because digital multimedia is such a new cultural form, there are few canonical references yet and it is still difficult to have confidence that everyone knows the cited examples.

Therefore I need to describe a particular example now, so I can focus my assertions. The example is a case study from my own practice-led research, a suite of digital multimedia projects called 'Life After Wartime' (LAW) that I've been developing with a team of collaborators from the mid-1990s up to the present times.[3] Responding to an extraordinary collection of crime scene photographs belonging to the New South Wales Police, the particualar iteration of LAW that I will cite here is a 'story-engine' or speculative 'conjunction-system' that restlessly combines still images plus haiku-like texts plus musical sound files plus stimulus from the interactive user.

The original archive, from which the LAW story-engine and all the other projects in the LAW suite are configured, is kept in the Justice and Police Museum (J&P) in Sydney. The Museum's photography collection is a rich cache of evidence associated with actual people who have been caught in painfully real outbreaks of fate, desire or rage. Most significantly, the documents that you would expect to be attached to the pictures – the conclusive texts such as the prosecution case, the defence case, the judge's summation, the jury verdict – all these documents are missing in the J&P archive. Each crime scene is represented by a dozen or so different photographic negatives swaddled in a tatty old buff envelope. Scribbled on each envelope, there is the name of a photographer, plus an often incomplete address plus a date and the photographer's guess at the crime being documented. And that's it, the full extent of the interpretive cues offered by the archive.

Therefore we have to work with a collection of files that are meaningfully but contentiously dishevilled, relative to one another. Because of the 'aftermath quality' of the pictures, we cannot help but proffer stories to account for them; but because of the dearth of accompanying information, we must accept that our accounts will always be speculative, restless and inconclusive, no matter how well informed we might be, historically, about the town and the times that produced the scenes.

After several years analysing how to use the images for a provocative and evocative street history of Sydney, the LAW collaborators have composed a volatile sound+image device that mimics and further stimulates the dramatic disturbance that plays in your consciousness when you encounter the photographs. This story-engine combines three reservoirs of files – images, caption-texts and musical sound components – all governed by relational attractions and repulsions that have been designed into the operating system: attractions and repulsions of image to image, image to text, text to sound, sound to image, and so on. Depending on what particular images the investigator chooses while the engine is throwing batches of pictures forward in turbulent patterns, the system gains cohesion governed by the history of each investigator's interaction with the database. Over time, a set of micro-narratives and mood-modulations accrue until eventually a kind of debateable meta-narrative builds up to account for the entire image-world of the archive. Crucially, each investigator will gather up a different set of micro-narratives and moods; and each investigator will tend toward a larger story in idiosyncratic and personally stamped ways. Each investigator will encounter qualities of themselves as well as qualities of the archive. In part, it is yourself you find when you delve into this interactive archive.

But it is yourself in relation to real patterned evidence shaped by a real patterned world.[4]

Engaging with 'Life After Wartime', you quickly deduce that you are not a reader or a receiver of this artwork. More precisely, you are implicated as an investigator. You are figuring 'what if' propositions, making postulative relations between elements and observing how those relationships play out, how productive they might be. Sceptically and imaginatively, you are making and interrogating a possible world even as you are attuning to an actual world of pre-existent meaning whilst also considering the authorial, compositional tendencies that work through and against your own interventions in the artwork's system.

'Life After Wartime' offers germs of stories which, simultaneously, you doubt and appreciate. With this sceptical yet postulative attitude, you wonder about the world that is witnessed in the pictures. You speculate about what might have happened in all the scenes. And you test those speculations against the contextually established knowledge that you have already assembled. In other words, you wonder and worry away at what you presently feel to be true for those scenes. You align your interpretations with commonsense beliefs, with what is already agreed to have happened in the represented world and with what the LAW system keeps proffering as possible interpretations. Again and again, without rest, you must speculate and test. You are never receiving a single line of interpretation. Although you sense interpretive patterns and narrative lines emerging and evolving, conclusiveness does not beckon. Rather, you are amidst an ever-blooming dramatic hypothesis that is always offering many different foci and perspectives even as you determine your own particular line of inquiry.

In this respect the 'LAW' story-engine is an instrument with which you continually strum ramifying chords in your mind – back and forth between memory and imaginative projection – so that an ever-developing concatenation of minor-key epiphanies can chime for you as you investigate and consider the ways to make sense of the seemingly endless power in the photographs. Colliding the images with breath-short texts plus changeful music and city noises, you cause all these elements to commingle so you can essay multiple liaisons and then disengage them before seeking again yet another spark in a chain of connections that might light up more portions of the occulted world that is represented by these crime scenes.

Speculate and test … essay and assay. The story-engine is meant to encourage this forensic rhythm in the imagination, the intellect and the spirit. It prompts a kind of divination. It is just one example of art made with digital systems. I think of it as a 'dramatic database'. And I think of it as a kind of aesthetic ecology defined by action contending with reaction, individual assertion contending with systematic resistance and adjustment.

Such artforms are beginning to abound now. Consider the popularity of the 'Sims' dynasty of fictive, faux-ecological environments. Consider too, the swarm of activity and debates currently energising the practice of architecture now that digital systems have become interlaced in all stages of designing and building. Once the convergence, divergence and emergence that characterise digital culture are made the central concerns for architecture (as they are for much of contemporary life), our buildings begin to look, sound and feel radically different. They *behave* differently. Ecologically. Dynamically. Like changescapes. Like much of contemporary life.

Responding to the dynamics of digital culture, such architecture can flex and alter according to the rhythms and aspirations of the times, according to the needs of its occupants. See for example, the active and reactive lighting systems that help buildings offer themselves to their participants in different ways in different contexts, for different crowds, for different purposes at different times of the day.[5] Built environments are now being designed as patterned, combinative systems (both material and informatic); they take the form of operable databases of elements that can be searched, combined and activated to create combinative complexes that unfold and re-align through time. And crucially this operability is beginning to be understood as the right and responsibility not only of the architect but also of the buildings' inhabitants (who are better imagined as *participants*).

Attuned to the logic of digital culture prevailing elsewhere in contemporary society, how might we best define such habitable, participant databases, such digital environments? They are dynamic systems comprised of light, sound, imagery and texts driven by code-motivated machines and reactive agents all relating and deployed in space and time. They are most easily seen in amusement parks, theatre stages, convention centres, flight simulators and crisis-management training centres. But they will soon be more widespread. They are buildings designed like multimedia programs, reflexively algorithmic contraptions or organisms that are always being reconfigured by variable energies, options, emotions and interrogations. More than mere settings or accommodations, they are continuous, designed *events* where preconditions, tendencies and reactions are encouraged to play out. They are always in process. They are changescapes. And rightly so. Let's not forget that the word 'building' signifies a noun-thing that is also an endless action energised by the verb inside it.

Once we have more buildings designed as changescapes, we should see more clearly that our built environments are actively composed from *conjunctions* ... conjunctions involving people, of course: engineers, architects, government officers, artists, merchants, journalists, general public. But there should also be conjunctions restlessly brokered amongst:

> stone, metal, other fabrics, reflected and refracted light, expansive and compacted spatial volumes, lines and colour-fields forming patterns, volumes of sound, activity and stillness, perspectives and obstructions offering stippling vistas for the eye so long as time moves along and so long as operating systems gather stimulus and make commands while inhabitants endlessly pursue their vectors.

We might understand that our built environment can be a communally-attentive multimedia system activated by digital capability and changescape aesthetics.

But really, why do the cultural forms facilitated by digital technologies matter? How do they warrant serious attention from aestheticians, systems theory specialists or writers of books? And why analyse them in the cultural-history context that I established earlier by privileging the approach pioneered in *The Rise of the Novel*?

Here is one answer: the operational dynamics and the recombinative readiness of the file systems in digital systems closely mimic the dynamics and recombinative readiness of contemporary post-industrial societies. This notion first chimed for me when I read Michael Joyce's cultural history of hypertext, *Of Two Minds*. Early in the book, Joyce observes that hypertext is special because it is a means by which we can prioritise structural thought over serial thought.[6] He explains how the cross-referencing and branching allowed by hypertext have arisen to serve a readership that is really a forensic audience, an audience looking to take charge of their own convictions, looking to *construct and test* rather than to *receive* their worldview. This is an investigative audience that knows there are many variabilities and volatilities defining life now, so many that it is implausible to rely on the reception of one line of argument or explanation (i.e. serial thought), because the premises on which any one serial discourse is founded are always debateable and subject to rapid redundancy. Instead, many people now are always looking to assess a multi-dimensional array of repercussions and possibilities associated with their every action in the world. No longer are people merely 'consumers' who are ready to accept the singular delineation of effect following cause following effect following cause. Rather, an investigative audience scans the field of lived and represented experience, assaying the strengths, weaknesses, opportunities and threats prevailing in the dynamic complex of tendencies, mutations and options that constitute the life of the somewhat free-willed subject today.

Or as the Indigenous Australian lawman David Mowaljarlai has described one aspect of the Ngarinyin philosophy coursing through his country in the Kimberley region of northwest Australia, people can develop a kind of 'pattern thinking' that helps them know and heed and tend the force that 'swings' in a place through time.[7] This pattern thinking is a determination to know the world dynamically, to know the ramifying, running pulses of connections amongst every component thing in the energised world. It is a determination to know *complexity*.

The etymology of this word is instructive. 'Complex' derives from the Latin 'plectare', to braid or plait. Thus when something is complex, it has many components and, crucially, these components come from *outside* the immediate configuration. When something is complex, it is receiving changeful, new elements and influences all the time. This makes complexity different from complication, which derives from the Latin 'plicare', to fold. When something is complicated, it takes on intricate patterns formed out of a complete, established fabric. With complication, old folds can be smoothed out and new ones tried out, but nothing elementally new comes into the system that is being manipulated. (Of course, intricacy can occur in either instance: complexity or complication. Intricacy: from the Latin 'tricare' meaning to puzzle or trick.) Hence, 'complexity' is the right word for grasping how ecological or open-system circumstances evolve. At any moment, complications are occurring in these complex circumstances – in these changescapes – but over time, new elements are always braiding into their systems and old elements are always leaching away, thus engendering the changeful complexity that is so characteristic when energetic circumstances are bounded only porously.

Digital multimedia systems have arisen partly to address the contemporary need for cultural forms that enable us to think and feel in synch with the volatility of contemporary existence. This volatility is complex rather than just intricate or complicated. Borrowing some phrasing from Michael Joyce, I contend that changescapes such as digital multimedia databases have arisen and become popular because they prioritise complex (or poststructural) thought over complicated (or structural) thought and over intricate (or serial) thought. Responding to the quickness and mutability of digital and transnational cultures, we need cultural forms that allow us to become sceptical and curious investigators of changeful systems. We need operable, speculative databases that surge with ideational and affective elements that can be searched, combined and activated to create complexes that unfold and realign, that evolve and devolve, that converge and diverge through time. And crucially this operability must be accepted as the right and responsibility not only of the author or designer but also of the participants.

To quote the multimedia artist David Rokeby (whose resonant theories we cited in an earlier chapter), with digital aesthetics one aspires to create *relationships* rather than finished artworks and one yearns to participate in systems which 'reflect the consequences of our actions or decisions back to us'.[8] To the extent that an interactive system is relational, cross-referential and meretriciously re-configurable, such a system is an aesthetic model of our dynamic everyday experience, our experience in the turbulent re-configurative world of globalisation, but also our experience in the delicate, complex world of ecological obligation, a world in which our responsibilities for our own environmental conviviality must be distributed relationally across space, time, class, nation, race, bio-habitats, gender and all the other seeming 'fixities' that once locked the West into a hierarchical armature.

More than just an informatic or technical tool, every multimedia database – even the most expedient or functional – is infused with aesthetics and semantics. Every multimedia database involves human-computer interaction and is therefore 'dramatic' and emergent somehow, because the interaction introduces novelty or change which challenges the established configurations of the system. Considered as an exemplary cultural form, the interactive multimedia database has a cultural history at the same time as it represents an innovative break with other representational forms such as the novel, the oil painting or the cinematic narrative. This cultural form has arisen to address the psychic and social dynamics of our times. It can be used for dramatic and aesthetic purposes, used like music, painting or cinema to tingle the intuition, to intertwine emotions and ideas, to conjure experiences of complexity and richness which help us reflect upon our everyday experiences as desiring and conspiring citizens.

Having wandered into this poignantly utopian position, can I get encouraged momentarily by the fact that database thinking is open-ended, investigative and restless rather than conclusive? Can I point out how we need theories that are informed by more than just linear-narrative explications and cinema histories when we analyse the cultural worth of digital multimedia systems? Can I suggest that 'fugitive' enthusiasms such as gardening theory, ecological philosophy, and even aquarium-design probably provide more useful kits of wisdom to help us comprehend complexity and contemporary social dynamics? As any gardener knows – Voltaire's Candide was not alone with this revelation – it is a complex enterprise to maintain an unruly plot of natural vitality with the bounds of a changeful cultural form. When you cultivate your garden, or your computer game, your digital databases, your interactive story-engines, you might find a safe haven where you can reflect upon the larger world.

## Notes

1. Ian Watt, *The Rise of the Novel: studies in Defoe, Richardson, and Fielding*, Harmondsworth: Penguin, 1963 (first published by Chatto & Windus, 1957), p.7.
2. Lev Manovich, *The Language of New Media*, Cambridge (Mass): MIT Press, 2001.
3. Kate Richards, producer; Greg White, programmer and sound design; Aaron Rogers, graphic design; Chris Abrahams, music and sound design.
4. See the website: www.lifeafterwartime.com
5. See the work of the Australian-based lighting designers Ramus Illumination, for example: http://ramus.com.au
6. See Michael Joyce, *Of Two Minds: hypertext pedagogy and poetics*, Ann Arbor: University of Michigan Press, 1995.
7. David Mowaljarlai, ABC Radio feature, <http://www.abc.net.au/rn/talks/8.30/lawrpt/lstories/lr311001.htm> quoted in Stephen Muecke,

*Ancient & Modern: time, culture and indigenous philosophy*, Sydney: UNSW Press, 2004, p. 172

8   David Rokeby, 'Transforming Mirrors: subjectivity and control in interactive media', in Simon Penny (ed.), *Critical Issues in Electronic Media*, Albany: State University of New York Press, 1995, p. 152

# 4

## COMPLEX DYNAMIC DISCIPLINES

In 1995, after a three-year period working as a consultant producer for the establishment of the Museum of Sydney (MoS), I began investigating a collection of 130,000 forensic photographs that had recently been stowed in the attic of the Justice & Police Museum (J&P). MoS and J&P are both properties of the Sydney Living Museums (SLM), a group of twelve museums, historic houses and gardens. So the evolution of the understanding that I am about to describe is part of a long-running collaboration between SLM and myself. I mention this connection to show how the research that I am analysing depends on relationships that flow in unpredictable ways across several collaborative teams, across several institutions and disciplines, across several domains of language, value and customary behaviour.

The J&P photographs were recorded by the New South Wales Police between 1890 and 1970. The pictures offer glimpses of life and death in Sydney over several generations. In these records we see a world full of yearning, folly and mendacity, a world as complex and mysterious as our own moment in time, but different. Most of the images are banal, many are provocative, and every one is mysterious, because all the written reports in the files were lost decades ago when the archive was rescued from a flood. There are no conclusive texts explaining the pictures, therefore, no prosecution case, no defense argument, no decrees of judgement, no 'last words' to put an end to the speculation that every image stimulates. The only clues are the inscriptions on the envelopes that hold each case-file: a date, a location, the name of a victim or suspect, a photographer's name, the photographer's generic classification of the crime under investigation.

Evidently, the pictures are not particularly useful for conventional historiography, but they are treasures for anyone interested in everyday life, in architecture, in gestures, fashion and vernacular ephemera, in historically informed speculation and imagination. So in 1998, sensing the profundity of the collection, I invited new-media producer Kate Richards to begin collaborating on a suite of projects that has grown to encompass a dozen artworks and two books plus seventeen journal articles addressing at least five different disciplines. This suite of works has become known collectively as 'Life After Wartime' (LAW). (www.lifeafterwartime.com).

Most of the LAW artworks have some computational and interactive aspect whereby words, music and sounds infuse the images in ways that respond to inquisitors' actions. In the artworks, narrative interpretations arise and proliferate. These narratives are loyal to historical research but they are fictional, associative and endlessly emergent. In this way the LAW projects are artificial ecologies that are fed by history in the service of contestable imagination.

All the LAW projects come from a collaborative process involving a team hailing from several different disciplines: algorithmic mathematics, computer engineering, industrial and graphic design, anthropology, creative arts, art history, history, museum studies, creative writing, sound design, musical composition, law and criminology. In order to rise to the challenges and opportunities of the LAW material, in order to make rigorous, speculative and affecting propositions with the photographs, the project team have had to understand the rationales and languages of at least a dozen different disciplines. We have had to learn how to blur the distinctions amongst these disciplines so that the team can together fashion new, shared argots; and we have had to learn when to insist on focused discourse that is derived from and stays confined to singular, constrained disciplines. If we refuse the disciplinary melt, we lose the nuances in the original material. But equally, if we abjure the disciplinary precisions, we cannot deploy the expertise that comes to the team through established modes of analysis and action. With the LAW works, therefore, we have to be both loosely polymath and stringently traditionalist.

One of the LAW projects is BYSTANDER. This is a large audiovisual environment driven by computers and sensors in such a way that the environment reacts to the behaviour of people who step into it. Depending on the attentiveness or distractedness of the visitors, the environment either offers coherent patterns of narrative and musical composition or it takes fright and 'devolves' into turbulence. BYSTANDER's audio-visual world mimics the behaviour of a complex, dynamic system. It is an interactive work informed by ecological precepts and by linguistic, narratological and cybernetic thinking concerned with emergence and complexity. Activating the profuse meanings and feelings that are poised in the evidentiary past, BYSTANDER encourages the involvement of a participant rather than the critical distance of a viewer.

Herein lies a great challenge to the scholarly disciplines that we have inherited. Most disciplines in the social sciences espouse dispassionate discernment and judicious assessment of carefully distanced objects. It is similar with the more critical strands of the humanities (notwithstanding the fact that 'affect studies' and the 'history of emotions' have become more influential over the past

## Complex Dynamic Disciplines

decade). But all around me now I see cultural phenomena and interactive relationships that are not objects, not stable or amenable to modeled analysis, not susceptible to distanced appreciation. Instead I see networked and interactive phenomena, events and potentialities that are complex, dynamic, relational and emergent. Computational projects. Online projects. Projects thriving on feedback from participants. These aestheticised events define my culture. My traditional disciplinary training is only partially useful for participating and intervening in such phenomena. Or more precisely, I see that I need to fossick amongst the extant disciplines in order to fashion some protean and involved ability, something engaged, unconvinced and not distanced, something that gives me a chance to understand what I am in when I create or encounter a work such as BYSTANDER.

Why do these interactive, ever-emerging and endless works matter? They matter because they give us a chance to sense how complexity works. Artists usually make interactive, immersive installations in order to create relationships rather than finished artworks, setting up emergent systems that 'reflect the consequences of our actions back to us'.[1] When you encounter such artworks, you get a feeling for the endless flux and paradoxically patterned unpredictability flowing in the world. The works encourage you to understand how you and the world are in and of each other, how you and the world are constituent of each other and mutually obliged. You are implicated, not distanced. Such artworks can help you know the complexity that plays out when individuals, their environments and their communities insinuate each other.

As I have already noted in a previous chapter, the philosopher Paul Cilliers has explained lucidly how complexity 'cannot be reduced to simple, coherent and universally valid discourses'. Not stable or objective, complexity emerges and evolves systematically.

To begin understanding a complex system, Cilliers observes, you have to get inside it, thereby diminishing your distance from it; then you have repeat the system and take note of its cardinal qualities, as they are discernible from the vantage-point in space and time that you presently occupy, paradoxically acknowledging that the system has altered already and cannot be repeated.[2] The quickest, clearest message you get is that you cannot reduce a complex circumstance to a static, schematic model separated from yourself. For complexity is relationally involved and always adjusting.

The drive to understand the dynamics of what Cilliers calls 'constrained diversity' is strengthening in contemporary culture.[3] Which brings us to the gist. Instead of producing a schematised blueprint or a critically distanced snapshot of experience, if you participate in an artwork such as BYSTANDER and you want to understand what is happening, you need to get involved and generate an interwoven set of narratives that encourage speculations about the endless dynamics of the system. In this way you become not only a participant but also a diviner, someone who proposes 'what if' scenarios; you pursue several ways to sense the tendency-governed changefulness in the situation. Delving inside the system whilst also maintaining a reflective vantage on it, you cross-reference the system's poised tendencies against your own history, activity and desires. And you observe and describe what happens while the system reflects the consequences of your actions back to you. In other words, you get a feeling for the way the system is tending, for its possibilities. And you constantly analyse and re-analyse this ever-emerging feeling. As fuzzy and ill-disciplined as it sounds, this heuristic attitude is true to the workings of complexity.

For Cilliers, the 'distinction between "inside" and "outside" the system becomes problematic'.[4] Complexity is not especially tractable to analysis, he explains, because the 'object' under analysis is altering from moment to moment: 'a complex system is not constituted merely by the sum of its components, but also by the intricate relationships between those components.'[5] If we map those relationships as an active network, 'any given narrative will form a path, or trajectory, through the network ... [and] as we trace various narrative paths through it, it changes'.[6] If we 'cut up' a complex system, we find that our 'analytical method destroys what it seeks to understand'.[7] Thus we need to treat all discernible patterns as momentary snapshots of contingent principles; then we have to take those principles back into the meretricious environment, knowing that the pre-set principles will soon fail or need adjustment. Once we sense those failures and adjustments registering in our analytical faculties, we are momentarily stalled again, needing to organise another batch of contingent principles which we then must take back into the system.

Inside – but also outside – but also inside. This rhythm is restless. And it's necessary. Because the world of lived experience is complex and restless like this; not simple, static or stable; not susceptible to schemas.

Being thus immersed and extracted, involved yet also critically distanced, ill-disciplined and shifty but also disciplined and reflective, you stand a chance of grasping both the world and yourself more comprehensively, not only more intuitively but also more analytically.

This is the paradoxical and re-disciplined capability that we need for finding our way through the complex world.

## Notes

1. David Rokeby, 'Transforming Mirrors: subjectivity and control in interactive media', in Simon Penny (ed.), *Critical Issues in Electronic Media*, Albany: State University of New York Press, 1995, p. 133.
2. Paul Cilliers, *Complexity and Postmodernism*, London: Routledge, 1998, p. 130 and 10 respectively.
3. Cilliers, p. 127.
4. Cilliers, p. 99.
5. Cilliers, p.2.
6. Cilliers, p. 130.
7. Cilliers, p. 2.

# 5

# THE KNOWN WORLD

## Introduction

Not so long ago, a brief memoir by the Austrian sociologist Andre Gorz became a bestseller in France.[1] *Letter to D* is a candid paean to Gorz's beloved and ailing wife Doreen, written while they both approached death in their ninth decades. As a history of a marriage, it is a romance of startling radiance.

More than a love letter, though, the book is also an investigation of what it means to know something worthwhile.

From Gorz's perspective, clearly the best thing to know is Doreen herself. But more than simply praising Doreen as an individual, Gorz celebrates the married mentality that they made together. Conjoining their distinctly different cognitive modes, the marriage of Andre and Doreen produced a coupled interrogation and account of the world, something that was more comprehensive than either of them could have found or made alone.

It is this epistemological aspect of *Letter to D*—in a register slightly different from Andre's lovely romantic hymn to Doreen—that I want to use here in my chapter on the conduct of research. For *Letter to D* examines the marriage of two offset but complementary ways of knowing. As Gorz contends, he and Doreen each predominantly enacted one particular mode of cognition respectively. There is no denying that these modes were stereotypical in their gender-ascriptions. But the typical roles that they first inherited and then challenged were part of the way each of them grew into the world and found completion during their particular sequence of European history.

Gorz had been trained in theoretical inquiry founded on a thorough understanding of analytical precepts and testable propositions. Using his inherited critical techniques as a political scientist, Gorz could stand at a contemplative distance from an object or phenomenon in order (i) to distil its galvanising elements and (ii) to offer prognoses about how all these engaged components might be driven or adjusted in lived experience. Accordingly Gorz addressed the world by referring first to all extant analytical accounts in history and then by proffering his own views for arguing and testing amongst his peers. His domain of knowledge was located mainly outside of himself and alongside the objects and phenomena being considered. To say it again, an optimal *critical distance* and a set of thoroughly debated precepts were obligatory to his mode of acknowledgement. His method was mainly discursive and objective.

Doreen, by contrast, tended to disregard the well-tested theoretical templates and morphologies when she addressed the world's enigmas and experiences. This is not to say she was uninformed or naïve. Rather, she would typically plunge into an experience as immediately and intensively as possible, choosing to abjure critical distance in the first instance. Whatever Doreen came to know of the investigated experience, Andre contended, she knew mostly at the level of subjective *conviction*, much the same way a great technician can have embodied know-how, but with a moral rather than a pragmatist tone to the cognition. Doreen's knowledge was dense and held close, couched in some entangled imbrication meshing herself into all phenomena being investigated. Whatever she knew, it was usually not critically distanced or communicable in received terminology.

Andre repeatedly found Doreen's insights to be compelling and *authoritative*. Doreen could make serious claims to knowledge, and even though it was shaped to the same worldly phenomena that Andre parsed, her knowledge was of a different order to the philosophically precepted understanding that Andre struggled to engineer. A different order, Andre averred, not lesser.

So the memoir acclaims Andre's understanding and admiration of Doreen's ability to generate lucid, emphatic opinions in response to actual experiences that had been palpably but also thoughtfully endured, absorbed and synthesized into robust conviction. He had learned over time that these opinions were knowledge. And he knew they had the force of wisdom in them:

> The authority—let's call it ethical—of such opinions does not require debate to hold sway. Whereas the authority of a theoretical opinion collapses if it can't convince through debate.[2]

Doreen drew understanding as directly as possible from her *experience* and in so doing she continuously unfurled a line of insights, starting in privacy before being decreed occasionally to the larger world, usually filtered through Andre's publications. By contrast, Andre tended to scoop together his pre-existing theories before carrying them repeatedly over to the experiences he was interrogating, so that in argument with himself and with other scholars he could observe how his extant theories might get shifted by the active, unruly world even as that world was always being knocked askew by the myriad beliefs that were always being applied to it. As he contemplated his marriage year by year,

Andre saw evermore clearly that the equal melding of the two modes of knowledge—his discourse and Doreen's ardently felt convictions—afforded them both a powerfully enhanced grasp on experience.

Assaying this marriage of two clearly different methods, it is evident that *Letter to D* offers important lessons for all kinds of scholarly research, particularly if we can learn first to imagine changes to the traditionally gendered roles that were foisted upon Andre and Doreen, and second if we accustom ourselves to the idea that one person can and should be equally adept at both modes of knowing, that one person can entertain both mentalities.

In this chapter I will be concentrating on research—which I can define quickly as the purposeful generation and communication of fresh and useful knowledge—that is pursued through artistic activities. But the knowledge generated should not be limited only to the arts. In any discipline or academic field that seeks fresh understanding in changeful circumstances, the notions discussed in this chapter should be applicable.

### Know this? First understand that.

Setting out to know the world better via art, we need definitions. We need first to define 'knowing' and 'art', so we can have convictions and debates (Gorz's two concomitant modes) concerning some roughly agreed fundamentals.

To know is to be in a state of having understood or comprehended something. To be enlightened against ignorance. Knowing—deriving from 'gnosis'—is a state of being imbued with some illumination, blessed with the ability to see into a mystery, to dispel the ignorance (which is the state of i-gnosis, the state of *not* knowing). Knowing is thus an after-effect of understanding. Literally, understanding is the process of bringing oneself close to the quandary, to stand under or in proximity to a mystery, to come in from outside its radiation and influence. By coming in and standing under the mystery, you can *comprehend* ('com'—'with'; 'prendre'—to take), you can literally take *this* aspect in hand with *that*; you can combine yourself with the mystery till you and it imbue each other and you *know* it with a glowing, gnostic sense of the rightness of your understanding. And then you need to know what it is that you know. You need to distil the principles of your knowledge momentarily, before using them as a way to re-enter the experience with more focus and brightness and with better questions.

Note the message that comes through emphatically here: you need to step both outside and inside the mystery. Not one without the other. This doubled compulsion will push through the rest of the chapter.

### Art is ...

So, if we are using art to chase knowledge via research, how do we define art, How do we know we are with it and in it?

Etymologically, art stems in part from the Ancient Greek word for to join, to turn, to round out and make complete. Hence 'arthritis'; hence 'articulation'. An artist makes a fulfilling conjunction and causes a turn in matter, time, space or events. This is why we evaluate art partly according to its ability to make changes in the given or perceived world. It is why great art is often felt to be transformational, even transcendent. So, here is my pocket definition of art to carry through this chapter: you know you are encountering art when you are engaging with an intentional process or product that causes surprising transformations for you in the ways you know matter or moments.

### Art as Research is ...

Research and art can join effectively to make knowledge whenever their conjunction causes a shift away from ignorance or befuddlement. The shift can often take you to a new set of befuddlements, of course. Even so it is *the shift in commonsense* and *the fresh ability to account for that shift* that ensures the occurrence is *research*. (Note: as many commentators have observed, you can do research for art, research about art and research through art. Mostly it is the latter process that concerns me here.)

Acknowledgement—the shift toward knowledge—is instigated when the researching artist conducts a productive and purposeful *experiment*. Etymologically, to experiment and to experience are closely related. (Indeed the French word for 'to experiment' is 'expériencer'.) An experiment – etymologically explained – is a venture through risk or peril. The experimenter goes consciously and interrogatively into and then out of an experience, veering at first into ignorance and then understanding the risks and learning from them, somewhat by immersion and then somewhat by exertion and reflection. Here is the oscillation between being inside and being outside, between 'being Doreen' and 'being Andre'. An experience is a dynamic and complex event that must be known through engagement with the organising tendencies within it and through attentiveness to the entropy and change also exuding from it. An experience is best understood experimentally, through trial and error, through a developing awareness of the actions and repercussions that are available and definitive inside the phenomenon that is being understood.

So we can now expand the quick definition of research that I offered earlier. Here is the chain of actions, reactions and outcomes that must be managed well in any productive research process:

## The Known World

the researcher **identifies** a need and defines a gap in knowledge attending to that need ⟶

the researcher collects all the extant information around the gap in knowledge, thereby surveying the field of everything pertinent that is already known ⟶

the researcher formulates a **method** and a set of experiments which will allow him or her to step from the known world into the mystery ⟶

experimenting, taking a risk to plunge into experience, the researcher **flows** along with the dynamics and complexities of action and reaction within the mystery until some **shift in understanding** has been sensed or observed ⟶

extracted from the experiment in that instant of noting the change, the researcher reflects on the experience/experiment, struggling for critical distance in order to **synthesise and espouse** some newly known proposition which can be drawn out from the fleeting hunches and implications of experimental studio-work until the proposition can be explicated privately to oneself first and then can be communicated to the scholarly world, the outside world ⟶

the scholarly community debates the claims around the new knowledge, and the claimant defends the claims persuasively until the proposition stands or is modified through discourse ⟶

the artist-researcher goes ardently back inside the experience, impelling the next step of acknowledgement.

## Experiment

Anyone who has ever developed an art project in a studio is familiar with those accounts of experiment and changefulness. This is why so much of an artist's knowledge always makes sense first as altered experience, as some inextricably *embodied* pattern of feelings on the move. The know-how that arises in the studio is immersive and nervous, more implicit than explicit. But for all that, studio-savvy is no less a form of knowledge than some other, more critically distanced mode of knowing. Anyone who has spent time muddling in a studio knows the value of this embodied savviness, this sense of tacit and delicate conviction in your bones.

(A quick explanatory note: obviously a 'studio' nowadays is not necessarily a set-aside room. It can be an online facility, a network or a laptop computer. For the sake of brevity, I will continue to use the word 'studio' in this chapter to signify the 'place' where the artist-researcher conducts the iterative, rigorous processes of experimentation which lead to new work and enhanced understanding.)

Given that the worldly value of scholarly research starts and finishes with how well and how widely any discovered batch of knowledge is communicated to a robust, discursive community of peers, how then can the artist-researcher's implicit insights and emergent understandings best be brought out and put about in the form of explicit and useful knowledge? Indeed, how much of an artist-researcher's energy should be expended on this question? Isn't the exhibition of the work sufficient? Why do some researchers (me included) insist that language—be it spoken or written—is presently a necessary component in the robust and effective transfer of knowledge?

The first answer stems from my recent experiences with government actuaries and multi-disciplinary committees. Accounting for the dynamics—informal as well as formal or policy-governed—ruling these powerful rulemaking bodies, I think it is currently imprudent to ignore the prevailing realpolitik. To say it plainly, I can report that scientists and most politicians are stunned and angered if an artist asserts that no linguistic accounts need to be appended to the outcomes of an experimental process. The scientists tend to offer a sincerely testy riposte: 'So, there's no need to write up our laboratory exercises—we should just let people visit the labs and everyone will understand all the nuances of what's being discovered. Everyone should just trust that we've made some breakthrough. We don't need to make our case?' In the next breath, they usually say that it is in the struggle to synthesise the lab-data into verbal propositions and evidentiary justifications that the crystalline and mind-changing precepts emerge. As one scientist said to me, 'First we have to learn how to manipulate *things*, then we have some chance of manipulating concepts, then we have to show what conceptual complex we can make from everything we have learned to manipulate.' At which point I can't see myself winning any argument about artists insisting on some privileged exemption from the demand for verbal disquisition and debate-based defence of knowledge-claims. There may come a time when a sizable portion of our society can sense and accept an artwork to be speaking directly and unambiguously to them in that particular artwork's own argot. Indeed most artist-researchers work to bring that time closer. But I feel the need to say this pragmatically, respectfully and strategically: now is not that time.

The second answer stems from my own experience as an artist-researcher, thirty years of which persuades me that although an exhibition might be an effective enough means of offering propositions to a small and stringently selected community of peers, there are undeniable benefits associated with the cognitive ordeal of hauling out and translating the implicit knowledge from one set of semantic and affective structures over to a linguistic set. This is because the explication coerces in the artist a series of cognitive shifts inside and outside the palpable and cerebral memories of the studio experience. In other words, the act of linguistic explication exhorts the artist-researcher to oscillate between (a) seeking the insider's ethical authority, derived as it is from studio-founded conviction, and (b) achieving the outsider's stance of critically distanced disquisition, wherein the validity and efficacy of claimed knowledge can be challenged and endorsed in extensive discourse. The linguistic explication does not 'decode' or 'explain' the work. Rather the explication opens an arena for debate around the knowledge that has been synthesised and proffered both in the work and in the linguistic account. The linguistic explication proffers one account of *what has been learned*. Thus by appending explicit oration to implicit know-how, the artist can cobble the doubled consciousness that Andre Gorz cherished at the end of his life with Doreen.

Why am I so confident that it is a beneficial ordeal to produce a linguistic account (*not* an explanation) of what gets learned within the ebbs, flows and pulses of artistically led research? The answer lies in the fact that artists typically investigate and shape dynamic circumstances. As they go about their work, artists experiment with raw matter or time or relationships amongst people, things and tendencies. In doing so, they can generate and convey knowledge about change. Usually this knowledge is tacit, unspoken, un-analysed.³ Conducting experiments to bring change to matter or to moments, artists work in the midst of complexity, thus catalysing mutability and making decisions about the best ways to find form within it. In experiments conducted in order to develop a work, the artist negotiates complex relationships of initiative-and-repercussion. Meanwhile, in the world outside the artist-researcher's studio, complexity defines everyday experience evermore emphatically in our globalizing economies. Given that most experts agree that complexity can be understood only by *experiencing it directly*, by imbibing and appreciating it from inside the systematics of its always-unfolding occurrence, then it follows logically that artists are specialists in this major aspect of contemporary life.⁴ In short, complexity needs to be investigated by means of a special, doubled mentality—a means of being fully attentive both inside and outside the unfolding phenomena—and artists are potential leaders of research concerning this paradoxical capability.

Infiltrating experience and reporting on it as an artist-researcher in this way, you might become not only a witnessing participant but also a diviner, someone who begins to distil brittle definitions about the tendencies that are pushing through the system, often in a covert or 'occult' way. Never actually predicting what will happen, never proclaiming that you have modelled any permanent templates underlying the system, you learn to propose 'what if' scenarios about the imminent and volatile future. You broaden your scope of *readiness* therefore, having developed the ability to be responsive to several possibilities surging out of the situation. You delve inside the system whilst also maintaining, quickly and restlessly, a reflective vantage on it. You put yourself both inside it and outside it.

Although these two modes of cognition are consciously distinct, they need to be occurring *almost* simultaneously, firing off each other so that you can experience a kind of intelligent shimmer arising in an optimal state of acknowledgement which the design theorist Donald Schon calls 'the action-present'.[5] In that shimmer you have the chance to describe the system's poised tendencies in such a way that you can then momentarily grasp your hunches about those tendencies and you can cross-reference these hunches against your historically constructed understanding of your own habits, desires, capabilities and states of readiness. Thus you get a motile but analytical understanding of how you and the world are dynamically implicated.

So, while you are observing and describing what happens within such complex circumstances, the system makes its own momentum even as it also reflects back to you the consequences not only of the world's stimuli but also of your particular prying actions. In other words, as soon as you sense how the system is tending, instantaneously you also analyse and re-analyse this ever-adjusting tendency so that over time, in the accrued account of the continuous dynamics of your own involvement, you get the best possible understanding of the ultimately imponderable workings of the system's complexity. Such an account of experience is a kind of research report leading to knowledge and some wisdom but never to certainty or prediction. ('Wisdom,' says Gregory Bateson, 'I take to be knowledge of the larger interactive system'.[6])

Here it is illuminating to re-quote and redeploy the ideas of Paul Cilliers, whom I have cited in earlier chapters. For Cilliers, none of the characteristics of complexity are especially tractable to analysis, for the 'object' under analysis is no object but an event that is altering from moment to moment: 'a complex system is not constituted merely by the sum of its components, but also by the intricate *relationships* between those components.'[7] If we map those relationships as an active network, 'any given narrative will

## The Known World

form a path, or trajectory, through the network … [and] as we trace various narrative paths through it, it changes'.[8] Thus, when we compile the narrative reports about what occurred inside the system, we accrue the best sense of how the system tends to go. The best sense—unreliable, uncertain but also somewhat divinable as you track the flow of tendencies.

How similar is this experience to the artist-researcher's daily business of experimenting in the studio! As Cilliers explains, if we pause to consider the flow of action-and-reaction in such an experience, we find that our 'analytical method destroys what it seeks to understand'.[9] Thus we need to treat all discernible patterns as momentary sets of contingent principles in motion; then we have to take those principles *into* the boisterous environment, knowing that these precepts will soon fail or need adjustment. Once we sense those failures and adjustments registering in our analytical faculties, we are momentarily stalled again, proposing another batch of contingent principles which we then take back into the system to see if they help us understand how all the dynamics are tending. Such is a good session in the studio.

The rhythm of this accounting is restless. And it is necessary, because the world of lived experience and discovery-based research is restless too, not simple, static or stable. Being thus immersed and extracted, involved yet also critically distanced, ill-disciplined and shifty but also disciplined and reflective—as in an artist's studio—you stand a chance of knowing both the world and yourself more comprehensively, not only more intuitively but also – and there's no denying that this seems enigmatic and illogical – but also more analytically. Regardless of whether we are scientists, writers or artists, this doubled and paradoxical access to knowledge is the re-disciplined capability that we need for finding our way through today's complex and changeful world.

Walter Benjamin, in his essay 'The Storyteller', recalls an old German axiom that can be translated as something like: 'when you have gone on a journey, you have a story to tell'. Benjamin explains that narrative prevails as our best means of accounting for experience.[10] Drawing from a life full of details (not only from his or her own life but also from a composite made out of the lives of all storytellers and their characters who have gone before), a narrator offers a web of insights about the tangle of causes-and-effects, actions-and-reactions, emotions and motivations that occur when someone ventures into a particular experience in a world of interconnecting contingencies.

Like Doreen's knowledge in *Letter to D,* the authority of a compelling storyteller comes across to the audience as a *conviction*, something grounded and ethical in its *persuasiveness*, rather than merely whimsical or dourly discursive. An authoritative account is a version of the world that seems to have been deeply experienced, lodged in the sensorium, known more in the bones than in the mind. At least the narrator's knowledge is implicit this way until it is explicated through the offering of a story that gives a report about the main, significant factors that impel the world that is being rendered in the tale.

So too, if you have been experimenting in a studio, you have a story to tell. You have journeyed into experience – perhaps into peril – and you have an account to offer about how the heuristic processes of *acknowledgement* proceeded through action and repercussion. This story of what happened in the making of the artwork is additional to the work that you can exhibit. Think of this account as a research report. It is the explication of what has been learned and earned as you ventured through the experience; it is the means whereby a scholarly community can be formed and all the tacit know-how that has been accrued in the creative process can be made somewhat communicable through language.

Once this communication has been proffered (accepting that any explication is really just a propositional flex of thought rather than a perfectly comprehensive translation of the artwork), then discourse amongst a scholarly community becomes feasible, because interlocutors can share language in order to contend with the outcomes of the research. In the best of cultures this discourse occurs not only in words but also in other artworks. In the best of cultures, we would be adept at extracting maximum intelligence from both modes of enunciation: from the aesthetic as well as the linguistic. And we would all be confident to draw on both.

And here is my concluding adage, which I offer on the basis of my experiences in studios and my investigations in books and conversations:

> Artist-researchers have the chance to woo two modes of knowing: the implicit and the explicit. They have the chance to entwine the insider's embodied know-how with the outsider's analytical precepts. The attraction between these two modes of knowing must be both felt and spoken. And as the world blooms in the artist's consciousness, the mutual commitment of the two modes can abide and provide.

At our best, we can set immersion and critical distance oscillating in a cognitive quickstep that takes us continuously and instantaneously inside and outside the dynamic experiences that we are always seeking to understand. Taking part in a venturesome, human culture of research and education, we artist-researchers may not be working to our full abilities just yet. We may not have brokered yet an habitual union between intuition and disquisition. But it is something worth facilitating. And the marriage of these two mentalities really does seem, at last, to be imaginable and achievable.

## Notes

1. Andre Gorz, *Letter to D*, London: 4th Estate, 2008 (translation by Julie Rose). First published in French in 2006.
2. Andre Gorz, *Letter to D*, p.59.
3. This notion of tacit cognition was well espoused several decades ago by Michael Polanyi. See his *The Tacit Dimension*, New York: Anchor Books, 1967. See also his *Personal Knowledge: towards a post-critical philosophy*, Chicago: Chicago University Press, 1958.
4. See especially, Paul Cilliers, *Complexity and Postmodernism*, London: Routledge, 1998.
5. Donald Schon, *The Reflective Practitioner: how professionals think in action*, London: Basic Books, 1991, 62
6. Gregory Bateson, *Steps to an Ecology of the Mind*, London: Intertext, 1972, p. 439.
7. Cilliers, p.2.
8. Cilliers, p. 130.
9. Cilliers, p. 2.
10. See Walter Benjamin, 'The Storyteller: reflections on the works of Nikolai Leskov' in his *Illuminations*, edited by Hannah Arendt, New York: Schocken Books, 1969.

# 6

## ATTUNEMENT AND AGILITY

'Globalisation', 'complexity', 'change'. These notions chime throughout this book. Now with this chapter I add some themes that are complementary but not identical. Namely, 'parochialism' and 'motility. The former exists in the shadow of globalisation; the latter is noise in the contemporary atmosphere. These terms will take us to 'attunement' and 'agility'. Four terms for the glossary. We'll see if they're useful.

First, parochialism. It has ecclesiastical connotations, but parochialism can be a secular term too, which is how I want to use it here. 'Parochialism' can describe a practice whereby you attend to a 'parish', a small administrative district that you know intimately.

It sounds simple enough. But we know such simplicity tends to be an illusion nowadays. Parishes were once presumed to be singular, their boundaries firm and agreed, and their concerns known and shared by the parishioners. But, consider any modern locality. Our places are agitated and activated by all manner of belief and power systems, all sorts of dialects, needs, fears and suspicions. We know that everyday life is stippled with contentions and incommensurabilities. We know this but we also simultaneously try to ignore it in order to get something done. (It is like how I write 'we' here in order to make an argument, despite how dubious we should be about sharing much in common.) Amidst the motility there is usually a yen to be 'grounded' and coherent.

The call for consistency and coherence is the chorus each of us sings, with good and bad faith, about what we know and how we want to live and work. But more and more these days, even if we try to operate parochially and are committed to knowing and fostering coherence in a place, we know too that the issues enlivening any place worth inhabiting are unstable, unsettling, complex. It's a kind of negative capability that you have to live with; a suppleness – which is not quite to say a shiftiness – that is always lubricating your inveterate, willing suspension of disbelief.

We know we live in *dynamic systems* rather than in *fixed structures* or time-frozen inevitabilities. (We *die* in inevitability.) Each vital moment is changeful, contingent on variable and unpredictable factors. With this changefulness understood, I hope it is clearer why parochialism is important: even as we need global connectivity in order to brace ourselves against the vicissitudes of contemporary economies, we know that a network holds together only so long as its local *nodes* – its secular parishes – are as strong as its outreaching tendrils. We know that sociability is simultaneously intensive and extensive.

So each moment is important and meaningful depending on how we conduct ourselves within an ever-extending panoply of semantic and social negotiations. Within networks. Each moment is *situated*, therefore, even though it is also distributed, relational and therfore shifty. Thus we know that we are in a post-structuralist circumstance, whereby meanings and messages are more negotiable than solid; we know that from moment to moment we can conjure some systematic sense at the very same time as, contrarily, this sense will tend away from stability, toward *alteration* while outside values and influences and ambiguous connotations press in around words, gestures, stances, statements and regulations.

## Attunement and Agility

Alteration: it is the process of undergoing change, of experiencing alterity or *otherness*. It is the process whereby you move through otherness and have it move through you, until you alter as a result of your encounter with difference, your encounter with products, processes and progenitors of motility. Alteration is contrary to stillness. Always in process.

Always in process. This brings us to *attunement* and *agility*. Instead of glossing these new terms etymologically as I have done with the other keywords so far, let me exemplify them by describing a scenario where attunement and agility must prevail if the scene is to have any meaning. Let's imagine a teamwork process, requiring collaboration.

The fact that we will need to *imagine* the process and its ensuing products is important: in a changeful world, the things that we create are somewhat without precedent, because the chain of events leading to the product will occur within circumstances that are complex. In a changeful world, imagining or *conjuring a possible scene* is the first collaborative action to be performed when people gather in quest of a possible outcome. To start a collaboration, some achievement, some thing or event or process needs to be held in your mind and shared with other minds in a 'zone' or 'safe haven' of possibility, in an encounter with strangeness, an encounter with something that does not really exist. This is the gas that has to get bottled: otherness … uncertainty … alteration … the difference between received reality and real possibility.

But I promised a particular example.

Let's imagine a project afforded by computational technologies and communication networks. Let's consider a landscape, something extensive and motile and complex, with a river system in its midst. This is a natural, social and sensory system. It has a plethora of smells, stories, actors, images, elements and urges in it, exiting it and entering it. It has social and historical patterns within it persisting through decades. It has batches of data gathered daily, gathered hourly, added to it in real time. Sounds, texts, measurements, images get captured, represented, transmitted into and out of it continuously. Inside this system, communities contend and combine. Power is there always disabling and enabling. Outsiders push in powerfully too.

Imagine the plenitude of data associated with all this activity. Imagine these data in their various formats all held as caches in different databases that are updating and sometimes breaking down, stuttering, freezing up or re-booting, minute-by-minute. Imagine how geographically and institutionally dispersed and isolated these various databases are likely to be. Now imagine what might happen if we found ways to aggregate these differentiated caches, all their different discourses, speculations, visualisations, descriptions and sonifications. Imagine too that such a system does not simply transmit or broadcast one-way to consumers, but that it invites intervention from several different constituencies which know themselves to be contributive and investigative rather than only receptive.

Imagine trying to set the conditions that would enable this system to come together. In such a project, you would need to broker combinations of the cultural, cognitive, aesthetic and political factors, to mesh with 'middlewares' so that a profusion of genres, individuals, legacies, communities could braid with different strands of government and systems of power, different valencies of affordance and impedance.

You might commence this brokerage all based on a *hunch* (which is an extensive, shared imagining, actually), a hunch that if you and your collaborators can amalgamate the right factors, you might start to discern unforeseen patterns and wholistic sets of relationships agitating in your environments and your polity. And this might help us know better how to behave, how to act and react in our dynamic systems when strange weather booms in, say, or when unexpected political actions occur for good and for bad.

So how would such a project come together in a situation where the amount of information, the array of protocols and the babble of languages are too profuse for any single mentality to contain it all?

One answer: collaboration, within changefulness, through *attunement* and *agility*.

By attunement I mean a patient and experimental process of listening and signalling, attending and altering. I mean the ability that we ought to have learned by now in the aftermath of colonialism, not to mention the aftermath of the internet. I mean the ability for all constituents to be in place through time with each other, amidst the different belief systems, habits and acknowledged variations of power, knowing all the while that there might be real mutual benefit in forming hybrid knowledge rather than in prescribing one knowledge at a fundamentalist, obliterative expense of another. Attunement is an ability to arrive at an effective frequency of informatic transmission. Think of what happens in ham radio sessions:

> signal … signal … response … poor response … signal … adjustment … better response … adjustment … stronger signal … stronger response … adjustment … attuned shared signal – resilient and sustained.

To attain a common frequency, one signaller and an other must move to an altered condition that gets negotiated and maintained via a wilful drift away from each signaller's initial, known frequency.

It is no innocent or value-free process, this attunement. For example, in Australia our colonialism teaches us that there is always a dominant key, even in social harmony, and that it is rare for anything like equity to occur when a powerful entity chooses to cede a little autonomy to underlings. No matter how much of a relief it might be, it is bound to feel condescending – if you are relatively powerless – when someone in power condescends to use less power on you.

This is where agility is vital. Amidst the negotiations and alterations, we need to ask how readily, how frequently and how *knowingly* can all the operatives *move* toward a shared level of possibility? Never denying that there are different degrees of freedom and 'purchase' in any particular collaborative opportunity, how might the collaborators still enact something creative and mutually beneficial?

The benefits come with the ability to improvise when change looms. And partly they come through *consciousness*, through acknowledging that the imbalances prevail and that agility is needed if the differences are not to paralyse our systems. Such consciousness can prompt us to practise attunement *for the benefit of the project* rather that for the benefit of any separate entity or group within the putative collaboration. It follows that if the project is delivered well and if the responsibility and credit for delivery are distributed truly, *the benefits* are distributed too. The world and its participants get something good that was not there before.

Utopian? Yes. Naïve? Not necessarily.

To show how complexity demands agility in a real-world drama such as business management, consider this typical scenario from ICT systems design:

## Attunement and Agility

In the creation of complex databases or elaborate communication and record-storage networks, it used to be standard procedure to deploy 'software engineering'. This might be summarised as the 'blueprint approach'. A 'top-down' process – executive and carefully constraining. Typically, with the blueprint approach, an organisation recognises that it has a challenging set of needs in relation to its databases and communication networks. It hires a specialist team to take care of the problem. The Board of the commissioning company is nervous, because plenty of money is about to be spent and competitive performance is at stake. So the Board takes its governance obligations very seriously. It insists that a detailed brief must be developed with itemised and milestoned 'deliverables' and that the progress of the project will be rigorously cross-checked against the brief and any departures from the brief will be penalised as variations or failures of delivery.

So, the consultant team spends a few expensive months moving through the organisation, asking everyone what they want from the new system. The people being asked do not necessarily know, nor do they know how the outside world is altering or what alternative IT systems are soon to show up in the marketplace, nor do they have the language, usually, to express any details. So the people being consulted ask for everything they can think of in as many emphatic phrases as they can marshal. Eventually a system is synthesised out of this process. More precisely, it gets described, scheduled and budgeted *on paper*, ahead of its creation. And the consultants set about delivering the thing that is detailed so starkly on paper.

Fast forward a few months. If everyone has behaved diligently and satisfied the Board's governance, the project has almost certainly proven to be an expensive failure.

For, in the intervening months, the world and the company will have altered markedly in the time between the scoping of the brief and the delivery of the system. And besides, the brief was founded in contradiction, ignorance, anxiety, babbled dialects and wild desire. Thus a complex and dynamic system was serviced by a structured mentality with faith in solid-state mechanisms, with expectations of social and moral fixity. The accountability applied during the development and delivery might have momentarily comforted the traditional anxieties of overseers, but these rigours were not aligned to the quickness of everyday reality.

Which is why the blueprint process has always been properly described as *engineering*. It serves rigid machinery. Instead, something like *atmospherics* or *fluid dynamics* would be more appropriate.

Alternative good-governance approaches have recently emerged for IT project-management, processes more attuned to complexity and motility. For example, consider the 'Agile Programming' and 'Extreme Programming' movements, which treat IT design as an iterative and definitively turbulent regime that constantly evolves whilst it continuously performs. A 'bottom-up' process – productively insurgent.

According to Agile Programming protocols, the design team is accountable to a rapidly churning but *planned* pattern of immediate needs and imminently useful developments. Or as the Agile Alliance explains its priorities in their online maifesto, they seek 'to satisfy the customer through early and continuous delivery of valuable software'.[1] If the 'scrumming' design-team can stay ahead of the churn, the system survives and the company even thrives because it is served by a dynamic process of evolution fueled recursively by actions and reactions, rather like a resilient eco-system. Accountability is then is a question of how well you have set the conditions for healthy change in your system.

Agile-collaborative techniques are by no means restricted to the ICT sector. For example, historians of architecture (and of governance!) might see how the Sydney Opera House started with Joern Utson attempting agility with his Scandinavian-atelier methods of research and deployment. Historians might see too how the project eventually collided with the solid-state, blueprint thinking of the New South Wales State Government officers who took over the project after Utson lost sway over his executive overseers.

If you work in a dynamic context – be it architecture, be it activism, be it ecology be it your family – you probably already know intuitively if not explicitly that your work proceeds best when attunement allows agility as well as accountability. As with many commonsense realisations, it takes some real diligence to draw this knowledge out of its implicit state and to communicate it as analysis and theories for future actions.

One way to embolden ourselves for this task is to see how these ideas about attunement and agility have precursors and are therefore quickly comprehensible because their precepts are already tacit or second nature to many people in our midst. For example, I see agility and attunement in the educational techniques known as 'heuristics', or discovery-based learning.[2] I see them in Polynesian wayfinding.[3] Sometimes in social-media aggregations.

In land-management regimes too, be they peasant, indigenous or ecologically scientific. I see them in many of the interpretive techniques of post-structuralist linguistics and textual analysis.[4]

And just to prove that such thinking is available to all political affiliations, I see agility and attunement in much of the corporate-research and wealth-creation philosophies propounded by marketeers like Michael Schrage and Richard Florida.[5] Ditto for the 'just in time' design-and-build protocols that now organise much transnational merchandising.[6] Ditto in the 'adaptive deployment' and 'swarm-formation' manoeuvres that are being researched in robotics and military labs all over the world.[7]

As cracker-barrel philosophers everywhere would insist: there's nothing new under the sun. True perhaps, but each new moment in history makes every next option strange and needful of creativity. And strangely, the best advice sometimes comes from the one you would prefer to define only as an enemy. After all, there's no telling where the next revelation might come from. How the alterations will bloom. For the sun has never shone *exactly like this* before, not right here, right now.

## Notes

1. See http://www.agilealliance.com/home or http://agilemanifesto.org or http://www.extremeprogramming.org/) (All accessed 12 December, 2014). These approaches to software design are somewhat informed, of course, by many of the ethical and intellectual tenets of 'open source' computing cultures all round the world.
2. See Zbigniew Michalewicz, David B. Fogel, *How to Solve It: modern heuristics*, Berlin; New York: Springer, 2000.
3. See Will Kyselka, *An Ocean in Mind*, Honolulu: University of Hawaii Press, 1987.
4. See Paul Cilliers, *Complexity and Postmodernism: understanding complex systems*, London: Routledge, 1998.
5. See Michael Schrage, *Serious Play: how the world's best companies simulate to*

*innovate*, Boston, Mass. : Harvard Business School Press, 2000. See Richard Florida, *The Rise of the Creative Class: and how it's transforming work, leisure, community and everyday life*, New York, NY: Basic Books, 2002.
6   See http://en.wikipedia.org/wiki/Just_in_time (accessed 12 December 2014).
7   See http://icosystem.com/releases/release_310502.htm (accessed 12 December 2014).

# 7

# CAMOUFLAGE AND CHANGEFULNESS

## Introduction

Over the past twenty years, many scholars from the various disciplines that comprise complexity science have provided insights into the emergent, *almost*-chaotic qualities that seem to organise large portions of everyday experience, be that experience physical, psychic or sociological. Sometimes the dynamic behaviour that such studies monitor is not immediately visible. For the changefulness that animates complex circumstances often occurs behind observable surfaces, in qualities of reality that are not optically explicit or instantaneously discernible. Instead the defining impulses might be found seeping in chemical, audible, haptic, morphological or olfactory dynamics. For the world presents and conceals itself in many facets and levels.

To the extent that changefulness characterises the world, therefore, and given that camouflage is an art for masking some patent characteristics of the world, this chapter asks how might an interrogation of the assumptions behind old and new camouflage practices challenge us into thinking in fresh ways about the complex systems and changescapes that host most contemporary occurrences?

It is generally agreed that because complex-dynamic systems are active and ever-altering, they cannot be usefully 'frozen' by analysts using prescriptive models, nor can they be conclusively understood. Complexity must be grasped contingently, impressionistically. Investigating complexity, one can best hope to get a feeling for what is going on using continuous narrative accounts, speculative animations and open-ended 'possibility charts'. To still these kinds of systems renders them no longer complex or dynamic. For as Joseph Margolis has observed, invariant objects are not necessarily the basis of reality, even though the post-Socratic Classical tradition (represented by Plato and Aristotle particularly) has long distracted us from the crucial pre-Socratic assertions (espoused by Thales and Heraclitus most notably) that everything depends on water and that the volatility of fire is at a core of all consciousness.[1]

Trying to keep faith with the live-ness of the world, therefore, this chapter seeks some fresh insights from the ways various processes of camouflage need to warp now when they align to the changeful systems of present-day experience. This is mainly an investigation of the given world, therefore. I have nothing much to say about camouflage itself; but I might be able to offer something *through* it, to say something about the phenomenal and unstable domains that camouflage tries to mask.

## Definitions

Camouflage is used for concealing. This is obvious. But can it be used also for revealing? Given that camouflage plays the apparent against the existent, we have a chance here to examine some basic precepts of sense-making. Rather than investigating what camouflage *is*, therefore, let's ask: what can be thought with it and through it? We can ponder what can be thought about the status of individual things; we can wonder to what extent things can also be understood as events when examined over time; and specifically how does an assemblage of event-things tend to engender communities, with all their structured but unruly characteristics? In other words let's ask what fresh insights might we generate, via camouflage, into individual sovereignty and psychology as well as into the communal systematics of politics.

To get started, we need to share definitions. First, what is camouflage? It is a process that encourages the misapprehension of something perceptible. By studying how this misapprehension proceeds, we stand a chance of grasping better how its opposite – apprehension – occurs. So camouflage is a prompt for re-thinking ontology and hermeneutics.

As Roy Behrens has observed, with camouflage most things tend 'to become less thing-like'.[2] The thing being camouflaged might be a haze of pulsing colour viewed as a shadow; it might be a loss of temperature; or some aromatic intensification. More than just a trick to the eye, most camouflage operates as an event, as a series of actions applied to objects and to intensities occurring in space and time. With their inherent changefulness, events tend to bring motion. And to quote Behrens again, thinking principally of optical duping, motion has always been 'the great spoiler of camouflage'.[3] Or to say this in other words, applying a contemporary focus: camouflage itself is changing nowadays, what with the preponderance of algorithmic tracking and emergent systems now making ever-altering environments which are supported and activated by ubiquitous computing and which old, static camouflage fails to mask.

Therefore motion and changefulness must be a major preoccupation for avant-garde camouflagists as they try to produce an ever-altering match for the shape-shifting that defines so much contemporary experience. Magicians, capitalists and camouflagists: it seems they all want to finesse similar kinds of transactional powers as they seek to extract advantage while matter and moments go morphing from instant to instant. To mask things as they evolve and devolve, as they emerge and submerge in patterns over time: this is the great quest of contemporary camouflage. The task is to track and trick conglomerations of things behaving together as unpredictable events.

As noted already, senses other than vision can be cajoled into misapprehension. Optical camouflage is just a sub-set of a larger venture. Indeed, even language can be understood as a camouflage ground. Irony, for example, is really a verbal and performative mode of camouflage. Many senses and many modes of sense-making – from the personal to the political, from the visual and proprioceptive or kinetic to the linguistic and intuitive – can get beguiled through camouflage therefore. And by examining these multi-modal duping practices we might know our sensibilities and consensualities in new ways.

## Relations

It is a commonplace to say that camouflage operates in the shimmer between figure and ground, between sense and non-sense, signal and noise, self and other. Moreover by focusing attention on the significance of *events*, we begin to understand how camouflage might also operate in the stutter between stasis and dynamics. Camouflage used to be principally a graphic and static form – patterns painted on boats, netting and screens blurring contours, and so on. But now it needs dynamics; it needs to be multi-modal, cinematic and also interactive, reflexive and emergent. This is because every present moment is always cohering while it is imminently disappearing in front of, around and within people who deploy the flourish of their senses for perceiving the nuances of experience. And these perceivers cohere and disappear somewhat too, as they attempt to sense the full store of relations that are possible between themselves (understood to be independent but also interdependent figures) and their shared environment (perceived and interpreted as shifting ground) all contending in space and time. Freedom flexes with connectedness, singularity vies with communality to make the structured but loose dramas that comprise sociability and politics, with the result being that experience arises in the simultaneously physical, psychic and social realm that we all inhabit, that we all try to influence even as it shapes us.

Speculating about what contemporary camouflage needs to be, we end up prying into politics therefore; into the commonsense understanding of integrated, communal experiences in a world full of motion. Speculating about the challenges for contemporary camouflage leads us to think anew about how the perception of things occurs through time, how this perception is necessarily changeful, ever-emergent and eventful, and how each perceiving individual has to be understood as a component or 'community-member' within the larger and shifting system that comprises experience in the phenomenal world.

Furthermore, there are machines now performing comprehensive surveillance for us and these machines, of course, can be duped even as they work to give the impression that we are well-served with vigilance. In such a context – human and mechanical – community can be defined as a volatile system of entities, a system that is not so much an object as an event insofar as society is an interconnected and contentious assemblage of interactors combining, recoiling, altering and unfolding as a perceptible phenomenon in time. And given that camouflage manipulates apprehension, we find ourselves asking: what must it track when its quarry is on the move and not entirely 'natural', when it is applied to systems – not only organic but also mechanical and computational – that are *complex and dynamic*? Answer: the camouflagist has to mask the apprehension of intricate and contingent *relationships* rather than (or in addition to) the apprehension of discrete and stabilized *objects*.

Poets have long understood experience thus. For example, the modern Japanese haiku master Seishi Yamaguchi based most of his career on an expansive idea that he borrowed from Stephane Mallerme: 'because objects are already in existence, it is not necessary to create them ... all we have to do is grasp the relationships among them'.[4] And Henry James, ruminating on the magic tricks required of a novelist, was similarly outreaching: 'Really, universally, relations stop nowhere, and the exquisite problem of the artist is eternally but to draw, by a geometry of his own, a circle within which they shall happily *appear* to do so.'[5]

## Fields and Lines, Grounds and Figures

So by speculating about the challenges facing 'eventful' or 'changeful' camouflage practices nowadays (recalling that camouflage has conventionally been 'spoiled by motion'), we have to think in fresh ways about what an individual actually experiences within the dynamics of complexity. The old camouflage theme of the figure-ground relationship is pertinent here, with the added intrigue that we come back to this dyad now knowing that the ground is rarely solid and the figure is almost never static or in focus or necessarily natural.

Recent studies in neurology are useful in this regard. For example Benjamin Libet's *Mind Time* proposes that consciousness is formed in a constantly arising-and-altering moment that is generated within each individual psyche as it negotiates the risky edge between itself and the larger world (which larger world includes, of course, oneself and other selves also).[6] This is another version of the figure-ground drama. For Libet, consciousness is comprised of a stream of present instants that coruscate in 'mind time', in an urgent, ever-evaporating 0.3-second interval of lived experience between when stimuli are first registered in one's broad-but-almost-formless awareness and then interpreted within the structured flow of inchoate, conscious personality. As these 'pre-conscious' stimuli are constantly processed within the 0.3-second intermission of burgeoning awareness, the present arises for each individual within the fleeting-unfurling 0.3-second interval; and socially the several individuals who comprise a community at any given moment more or less agree that experience is unfolding in synch for them all. This is how long the present lasts: 0–0.3 seconds.

At a social level, the present moment is a kind of structuring fiction that normally allows us to get on with acting while each person's emerging consciousness is extracted, instant by instant, as a line drawn out of time from the deep, volumetric flux of threats and opportunities that constitute existence in a vast world of phenomena and stimuli. Libet's experiments show that for every human being attempting to make his or her particular way through the engulfing world of threats and opportunities, the brief 'moment' of less than half a second lets the individual scan for information before beginning consciously to interpret the raw stimuli; in other words, the individual scans for threats and options before asserting the figure of itself against the ground of the shifting stimuli.

This scanning-process is a rapid-fire, continuous 'snapshotting' of everything perceptible. It is a survey of the fecund 'ground' from which the figure of one's consciousness must step and step again and again. The snapshotting is wide-angle and non-hierarchical, because all threats and opportunities must be treated as equal until interpretation offers shape to the data and gives sequential actions a real urgency in a kind of survivalist 'workflow' or story-line. Interpretation is thus 'figural' because interpretation is the application of structure on the basis of your memory prompted by your extant personality while you monitor the profuse array of possibilities or prospects that will emerge from the ground where you have retrospectively stored your past experiences. The self draws a line out of the ground. Memory, desire and imagination jostle to make a contest with fate, all of which produce perceptible experience. Thus consciousness arises even as it stumbles. The self lives in a kind of shimmer where a somewhat-formed figure jigs in the ground of the messy world. We can understand this drama of consciousness, therefore, as an event performed in *a field* of received experience out of which *a line* of enacted sovereignty is drawn by each conscious subject. The line is drawn by the conscious figure; the field is delimited in the larger ground of worldly experience and memory.

Iain McGilchrist's *The Master and His Emissary* presents a comparable worldview.[7] McGilchrist explains how the 'bi-cameral' brain, with its symmetrical but differently operational halves, offers the chance for each conscious mind to be formed in a dynamic oscillation between right-brain and left-brain predispositions, between hyper-observant contingency-scanning and super-efficient prescriptive processing. Pattern-apperception combines with narrative-imposition. Although most people and cultures tend to be dominated by one or the other of these two dispositions, McGilchrist contends that the most vibrant and capable consciousness maintains its best stability almost gyro-scopically, by actively oscillating the two modes, each around and through the other, so that the world is perceived and interpreted both extensively (as an open field of contingencies) and intensively (as assured lines of prescribed reasoning and narrative). Figure, ground, focus, breadth, change, adaptation, action, alteration, emergence: consciousness and the vast, immanent world chase each other through these turnpikes.

## Connectedness and a Conclusion

With astonishing prescience, Ralph Waldo Emerson saw it and said it vividly in the 1840s:

> Really, all things and persons are related to us, but according to our nature they act on us not at once but in succession, and we are made aware of their presence one at a time. All persons, all things which we have known, are here present, and many more than we see; the world is full … No sentence will hold the whole truth, and the only way in which we can be just, is by giving ourselves the lie; Speech is better than silence; silence is better than speech; — All things are in contact; every atom has a sphere of repulsion; — Things are, and are not, at the same time.[8]

This is how we can be goaded into re-thinking and stretching our solid-state models of the world: by considering what camouflage really needs to be. Sensing the limits of good duping, we can sense too the duplicity of the solid old world. Which is where the examination of camouflage can lead us: into fresh considerations of the ways we understand in relation to phenomena even as we know ourselves just to be phenomena.

So camouflage might help us apprehend afresh how every figure really does seem to stem from water even while it yearns to be on solid ground. Every thing that seems solid wants to absorb each of its others. The figure and the ground give rise to each other.

## Notes

1. See Joseph Margolis, *The Flux of History and the Fux of Science*, Berkeley: University of California Press, 1993.
2. Roy Behrens, Public Keynote Lecture, *Camouflage Cultures: Surveillance, Communities, Aesthetics, Animals*, an international conference and exhibition co-convened an co-curated by Ann Elias and Nicholas Tsoutas, Sydney College of the Arts at The University of Sydney, 8 August 2013.
3. Behrens, Keynote, *Camouflage Cultures*.
4. Seishi Yamaguchi, 'Preface' to his *The Essence of Modern Haiku*, Atlanta: Mangajin: 1993, p. xix.
5. Henry James, 'Preface' to his *Roderick Hudson*. (The novel was first published by James in serial form in the *The Atlantic Monthly* in 1875. The 'Preface' was first published by James in 1907). See the online creative commons version: http://www.henryjames.org.uk/prefaces/text01.htm
6. Benjamin Libet, *Mind Time: the temporal factor in consciousness*, Cambridge (Mass): Harvard University Press, 2004.
7. Iain McGilchrist, *The Master and his Emissary*, New Haven: Yale University Press, 2009.
8. Ralph Waldo Emerson, 'Nominalist and Realist', in *The Complete Prose Works*, London: Ward, Lock and Co., 1891, p. 150. (First published in 1844.)

# 8

## NARRATIVE HUNGER – GEOGRAPHICAL INFORMATION SYSTEMS, GOOGLE STREET VIEW AND THE COLONIAL PROSPECTUS

*Flat as the table*
*it's placed on.*
*Nothing moves beneath it*
*and it seeks no outlet.*
*Above – my human breath*
*creates no stirring air*
*and leaves its total surface*
*undisturbed.*

'Map' by Wislawa Szymborska[1]

There are millions of maps like the one Wislawa Szymborska describes. But in this essay we will be looking at another kind: geographical information systems, which *do* get stirred when people engage with them. Arrayed on screens, the surfaces of these interactive maps are designed to be unsettled. Electricity and data-accrual agitate them, letting them change with context and consultation. They are still accounts of space, these new kinds of maps, but they are not placid. Still maps but not still. They alter from moment to moment, tracking time, gathering a record of everyone who visits them, who gets folded into them.

When users are continuously updating a map with personal details and storylines, it is no longer the old Cartesian thing we

## Narrative Hunger – Geographical Information Systems

thought we knew, no longer an abstract and rigidly coordinated arraignment purporting to offer disinterested orientation by addressing every surveyor equally and objectively. Once you have become a participant and have etched some of your experience into a cartographic system, thereby changing it with your actions, the system is dynamic, reactive and not separate from you. It is not simply an object to your subject. It is not the flat thing Szymborska scrutinises.

Moreover an interactive map stores a *narrative* that involves you as a character. With each new recorded visitation from you, the narrative grows around your character. And while you might want to regard this first-person figure as the protagonist in the mapped setting, you know in fact that computationally you are no more special than the myriad other data-packages – animal, vegetable, mineral and commercial – that make up the network that you are negotiating.

See how ruffled and protean the new mapping system really is? This notion of an *active mapping network* plainly disturbs the two orthodoxies that have customarily contended in the definition of cartography: namely, the map as a perspectival setting for narrative and the map as an invariant abstraction that coordinates fixed information. More about these old contenders, presently.

As Laura Kurgan explains in her impressive book *Close Up at a Distance*, when we interact with digital geo-location systems 'we do not stand at a distance from [the] technologies'. Rather we 'are addressed by and embedded within them'.[2] In her role as Director of the Spatial Information Design Lab at Columbia University, therefore, Kurgan has been pursuing research projects that:

> explicitly reject the ideology, the stance, and the security of 'critical distance' and reflect a basic operational

commitment to a practice that explores spatial data and its processing from within. Only through a certain intimacy with these technologies – an encounter with their opacities, their assumptions, their intended aims – can we begin to assess their full ethical and political stakes.[3]

They are maps too, of course, the computational systems interrogated by Kurgan; but not as the West has preferred to know cartography for at least six hundred years. The received wisdom is that maps locate the world for us, that they are stable and dependable out in front of us. You can read them as if they offer a natural language because, explains Kurgan, from the earliest explorations in which you used maps to find your way and assert your agency in the wide world, you have absorbed and appreciated the efficacy of all their 'conventions, ranging from their legend, scale and codes of graphic representation to what counts as the information that they represent' as they give you 'a system of notation or coordinates that places things in relation to one another'.[4]

When these traditional maps serve so well, they do not seem to deserve interrogation, doubt or disturbance. They take you places; so why not just endorse them, treat them as natural, and carry on? Which is another way of saying that the classic Cartesian map gives the viewer the privilege of hovering potently outside its chart; no participant breath shifts the well composed data; the array is set to be trusted as constant and clarifying.

We know this implicitly and most people accept the solid-state coordinates comfortably. But with Kurgan's help, let's not dodge what we have come to understand since our phones got smart and started talking amongst themselves while we carried them around:

## Narrative Hunger – Geographical Information Systems

This drive to locate, to coordinate, however revelatory and even emancipatory it can be, also has its price. It seems as though in the end, maps – the successful ones, the ones that show us where we are and get us from here to there – risk offering only two alternatives. They let us see too much, and hence blind us to what we cannot see, imposing a quiet tyranny of orientation that erases the possibility of disoriented discovery, or they lose sight of all the other things that we ought to see. They omit, according to their conventions, those invisible lines of people, places, and networks that create the most common spaces that we live in today.[5]

So what happens if you take one of Kurgan's more quixotic provocations seriously, once you have paused and considered how all people with phone accounts have some access to the interactive datascape even as they contribute to its massification? Kurgan puts it like this:

The word 'data' … means nothing more or less than representations, delegates or emissaries of reality … not presentations of things themselves but representations, figures, mediations – subject, then, to all the conventions and aesthetics and rhetorics that we have come to expect of our images and narratives. All data, then, are not empirical, not irreducible facts about the world, but exist as not quite or almost, alongside the world; they are para-empirical.[6]

In response to such provocations, what might happen is that you could step off from your 'comfortable sense of orientation, of there being a fixed point, a center from which we can determine with certainty where we are, who we are, or where we are going'.[7] And by doing so you might comprehend yourself not as a sovereign point blessed with an executive overview of a conclusively quantified and invariant field, but rather as a flowing, ever-contingent and shifting intensity within an extensive relational network. You could begin to know a world in which change is definitive rather than regulated into charted stasis. The coordinates that Cartesian systems install against doubt and contingency would float more freely. Relativity would abide instead. For good as well as for dread.

Kurgan's provocation is to 'put the project of orientation – visibility, location, use, action and exploration – into question … [but] without dispensing with maps'. Thus you might get a more telling access to everyday reality as it actually rumbles – the world as it *is* rather than as we might wish it to be. To finish this thought and to agitate the solid world, Kurgan borrows a tenet from the art historian Rosalyn Deutsche, declaring that perceived reality is actually 'constituted in a complex of representations' which realign and re-charge constantly, depending on the valences operational at any particular time and place in the network.[8]

Kurgan works a canny gambit to get us used to interrogating this 'project of orientation'. She displays two NASA images of Planet Earth: File AS8-14-2383 which is popularly known as 'Earthrise'; and AD17-148-22727 which is celebrated as 'The Blue Marble'. These public-domain pictures, with their striking backgrounds of deep-space black, are usually celebrated as gorgeous colour studies. They have been printed out and posted up to bring cheer to countless dorms and bedrooms. The tasty foreground of musks and greys in the first photo offsets the chilly blue abstractions of the second. But for the cartographically inclined, the important difference is that one image is a landscape which acts

## Narrative Hunger – Geographical Information Systems

as a narrative setting and the other usually gets regarded as a map of Africa.

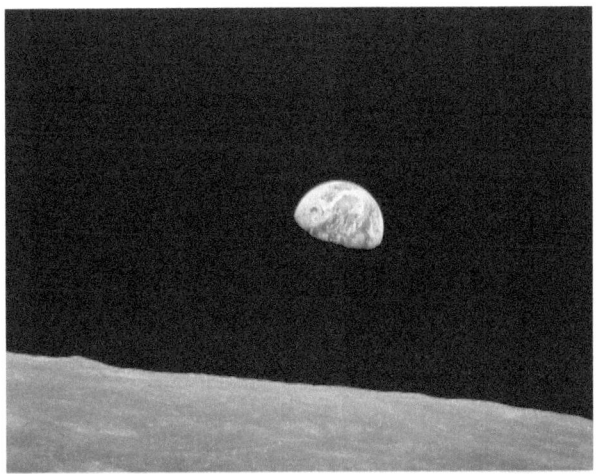

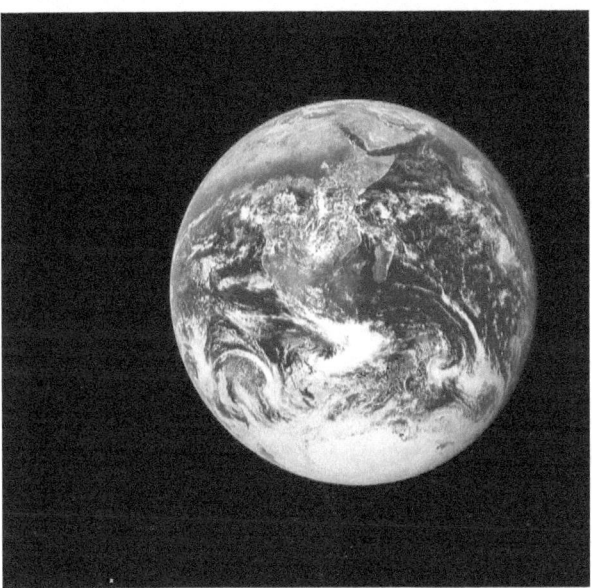

Addressing a protagonist standing sovereign at the apex of its scene, 'Earthrise' offers a perspectival track into a journey – how did you get here on this lunar plain and where are you about to go? 'The Blue Marble', however, displays the 'total surface' (to invoke Szymborska again) of the planet's primordial continent and it hovers you nowhere, without a particular standpoint. The first image involves you in a particular narrative, suggesting possible trajectories for yourself, foreground to yonder; the second extracts you into generality, offering an empirical, Cartesian assay of space outside you. In this difference between the two images – the poetics of a first-person narration versus the empirics of an encompassing survey – we have a distinction that helps us understand the animus of contemporary mapping. With 'Earthrise', you are *in and of the scene,* intensified and in process in a landscape that hosts a story right now for you. With 'The Blue Marble', all the information you need is *over there,* in that contained and quantified object.

Which brings us back to Kurgan's interest in the collapse of critical distance, seeing that a landscape, a Cartesian map and a metadata-rich information-network are all spatial somehow but by no means commensurate. It is this move away from the 'locked-off' edition of Cartesian mapping – the 'total surface undisturbed', as Szymborska calls it – to the landscape-view of journeys traced *into continuously updating feedback systems* that is presently redefining how maps are made and used.

Pinging satellites have allowed a more axonometric kind of view that re-locates the viewer as surveyor from the affectless hover-point above a map to something more like witness-proximity. To this end, Kurgan features (and pays for) a striking image in her book. She describes it as follows (and it is well worth finding online; for example at: http://www.space.com/12803-september-11-anniversary-attacks-space-photos.html):

> a one-meter resolution satellite image of Manhattan ... collected at 11.43 a.m. EDT on September 12, 2001, by

## Narrative Hunger – Geographical Information Systems

> Space Imaging's Ikonos satellite. The image shows an area of white dust and smoke at the location where the 1,350-foot towers of the World trade Center once stood. Ikonos travels 423 miles above the Earth's surface at a speed of 17,500 miles per hour.⁹

Can you feel the vertigo and the narrative poignancy that springs from the plummeting vantage-point? There is a column of vapour gyring up toward you that is a bridge between the abstract world of mapping and the closely-felt testimonial world of time-coded and landscape-set storytelling. You can almost smell it. This poignant index of an actual event – which occurred in real time in a space you can visit – shifts the image back and forth between map and scenario, between information and all the emotion-laden complexity that stories carry even as they also freight and delineate great loads of data.

With all this melding of scene-setting and mapping, the paradigm-shifter has been Google Street View, which links 'on-the-ground' landscape-renditions to traditional coordinate-charting via Geographical Information System (GIS) surveys and networked user tracking. At will you can move yourself inside and outside the scene, then back inside again, and so on, blending distance and involvement within a mode of knowing that is both intensive and extensive.

Try monitoring yourself as you work with Google Maps. Most likely you will start by typing a location-search. These words will give you a schematic map that you can change into a zoom-able satellite view before you go back to the map in order to activate Street View. At this moment you get folded into a grounded vista, 'travelling' and narrating along perspective-lines that you select within the 360-degree half-dome of vision that is availed by your cursor-clicking within the website. And all the while, you know that you can float out to abstraction again at any moment, to hover at a critical distance outside the 'total surface' that is always offered by the Google Map schema, as distinct from the Google Earth setting or the Street View trajectory. Inside, outside, inside, and so on.

For me, the most striking aspect of journeys taken along Street View's seemingly infinite itineraries is the 'narrative hunger' they stimulate. I fashion this term from David Shields' popular study of non-fiction writing *Reality Hunger,* in which he accounts for the amplifying interest in witness-reportage.[10] With a *narrative* hunger, I suggest, viewers encounter a setting that compels them to scan for cues about what to feel and what to tell in response to the scene. The hunger intensifies if the scene befuddles or if it fails to divulge, if the viewers *find no reliable cues*, nothing semantic or affective to prompt a satisfying story. Coming up empty, lost in blankness, the viewers know narrative hunger. And they may respond with utterance.

Go travelling with Street View. You will see what I mean. The blankness emanates from the aesthetic qualities in each image but also from the automated rhythm of image-capture as the Google Car trundles along. The 360-degree Google Camera makes no subjectively nuanced selection with each framed and snapped image; it just operates indiscriminately all around itself on clock-time. It simply blinks and plods on. Vernacular parlance has dubbed it 'zombie-cam'. This nickname evokes well the amorality of the images. But I would like to add 'stumble-cam' to the lexicon. For it is as if the mobile camera is concussed and unfocused as it travels, thoughtless and uncaring, on auto-pilot, nothing invested. As it moves implacably into the landscape, the Google Camera gobbles up a vast territory of future prospects.

## Narrative Hunger – Geographical Information Systems

It stitches no obvious stories into its journeys, but it lays out a plethora of settings in anticipation of future values that could be poured into them.

In this regard, the journeys of the Google Camera are prospectuses awaiting 'investors', be they monetary speculators, be they narrators. Of course, there are thousands of projects online that have been roused by the narrative hunger. A profusion of artists, for example, have poured significance into the blank scenes, offering narrative texts, providing soundtracks and musical cues, or selecting poignant images that lift the viewing experience out of the automatic daze that zombie-cam engenders.[11] But overall the daze prevails. Image-sequences in Street View almost always arise with a rhythm that feels somnolent rather than pointed, pre-destined or sovereign. In other words, there is currently not much triumphalist colonialism or energetic modernism on display in Street View. (Which is not to say the system will always be so wide open, so blank and multi-valent.)

In the myriad post-colonial scenes of sociological and ecological devastation that the Google Car has captured all around Australia, for example, one cannot help but feel that the sovereign viewer has been rendered catatonic somehow. There's been a shift of gears. Centuries of manifest destiny and perspectival privilege have led to lostness, to paralysis, to a befuddlement about where you can drive next for satisfaction or profit. Perhaps this is melancholic: the cessation of movement. Or perhaps it is optimistic: the call for a surge in new kinds of spatio-temporal encompassment and *involvement*.

It is the process of moving through the landscape – specifically of moving for the purposes of *surveying and mapping* – that demands and rewards our attention here. John Barrell, in his 'landmark' books *The Dark Side of the Landscape* and *The Idea of*

*Landscape*, offers astute guidance for this topic, with his canny analyses of rural politics and poetics in early-industrial England.[12]

Barrell examines the assault that fell upon the commons during the Eighteenth Century when land-tenure was forcibly altered across most of Britain so that extensive tracts that had long been held, farmed and husbanded communally, in a 'traditional' way, were transformed to become intensive, enclosed estates that were owned personally, sequestered and exploited, in a 'modern' way. Barrell shows how the twinned phenomena of the Industrial Revolution and the Agricultural Revolution coincided in Britain not so much because farming was revamped by the invention and sudden availability of new machinery, as has been long surmised. Rather a change in *mentality* probably occurred first throughout the most powerful section of the populace, Barrell contends, causing a cultural change that encouraged landgrabbing and the adoption of an entrepreneurial attitude to estates. Which led to the countryside being treated as an object full of raw materials and natural resources. Among the class of men who realised they could exert their influence, the rural world was redefined as an agricultural object that could be processed with the efficiency afforded by the mechanical advantage and energy-transfer that were the drivers of the Industrial Revolution. The change in the culture governing farm-tenure brought a reason for the industrial 'barons' to lock on to rural economies as well as to urban factories.[13]

As they acquired portfolios of estates, the new landed speculators became owners rather than tenders. No longer was it obvious that a person should come from and *belong to* one particular place. And someone who owns many places can quickly become accustomed to the idea that it is good to *move through* these places and to move from place to place as a celebration of personal sovereignty. These parvenu property-owners were part of a new 'rural professional class ... whose interest in the land was not primarily aesthetic', who were 'accustomed, by their culture, to the *notion* of mobility and could easily imagine other landscapes'.[14] They had found a modern, industrially efficient way to encompass the spaces that they had requisitioned, reaped with a mobility that afforded them a kind of proprietorial ubiquity. I am reminded here of Michel Serres' observation that 'the Romans built the Pont du Gard less for the purpose of transporting water by aqueduct than for the purpose of demonstrating their power to the local population'.[15]

It is a simple next step to regard all land as matter waiting to be landscaped. In this process every representation of the countryside quickly appears like a profiteer's prospectus, like an offer to convert raw or natural resources to product and property. For good and for bad, Google Street View is the latest phase in this long march across the planet's territories. In Australia, with Google's extensive photographic coverage of the continent's vastness, Street View mapping allows a mode of virtual travelling that feels like free and benign browsing, as if the intensively enclosed territories of the gridded world have been opened up and held in common again. (That little Google Car has been to an extraordinary proportion of Australia; not just to the cities and suburbs, but along tens of thousands of dirt tracks and corduroy roads that very few citizens have ever traversed.) But dating from 1788, when the first colonising garrison was established at Sydney Cove, there has been a long and troublesome history of this style of movement, this 'prospectus mode' of hungry mobility.

In post-1788 Australia many of the explorers and settlers who forged into the landscape published travel accounts. Or more precisely, they produced *traversal* accounts. Celebrating acquisitive movement in the way Barrell has explained, these accounts compiled inventories that assayed a vast stockyard. The accounts were guide books for prospective entrepreneurs looking to launch their ambitions across new fields of profit. Of course, the newness of the terrains could be credited so long as the traversers did not tarry to witness the methodical land husbandry performed by Indigenous custodians, so long as the traversers declined to note that the entire country was already braced with infrastructure and design that had been made and maintained during centuries of native diligence. In this sense, all the traversal tales, even today's, are colonial prospectuses, tabulations of assets and entrepreneurial opportunities. Self-assertion and continuous acquisition, rather than communal and ecological custodianship, are paramount in these traversal ventures.

Consider this bravura example from the middle of the 19th Century, a whooping paean to territorial mobility. It was published by Major Thomas Mitchell, first Surveyor-General of New South Wales and keeper of the colony's cadastral records. Mitchell reminisces about an invigorating day exploring a wild tract out past a hamlet's edges:

> The calls of the natives, first heard at a distance in the woods, having become more loud, and at length incessant, I answered them in a similar tone; and having halted the carts, I galloped over a bit of clear rising-ground, towards the place from whence they came.[16]

Such momentum carries Mitchell imperially as well as imperiously:

> We now advanced with feelings of intense interest into the country before us, and impressed with the responsibility of commencing the first chapter of its history. All

was still new and nameless there, but by this beginning we were to open a way for the many other beginnings of civilised man and thus extend his dominion over the last holds of barbarism.[17]

Motoring forward one hundred and fifty years, I think it is not too fanciful to regard the *Mad Max* films as part of this cultural tradition. Actually, the films are critiques rather than continuations of the mania for mobility. With their dystopian vision of what the urge to roam and rule can produce, they play out a scatologically thrilling endgame for voracious momentum. Offering a raucous completion to the hollering that Mitchell initiated, the films have struck a chord with massed audiences for more than thirty years, from the period of their production when the oil crisis and ecological collapse first smacked into popular consciousness worldwide. They drive the imperial tale of acquisitive traversal to a mad kind of apogee. They are hypercharged with an explicit narrative mission: ride the white line fever to a flaming climax. This is unequivocal. The viewer needs not supply any extra meanings or thematics.

By contrast, what is striking about the road movies that Google Street View supplies is that the narrative assertion driving the *Mad Max* films has evaporated from the landscapes. Even while it takes account of tracts of land that can be tagged as data to be leased out as a type of real estate – much as Thomas Mitchell did when he published his journals – the Google Car seems stuck in first gear, so unlike the muscle cars in the *Mad Max* films. Indeed, so unlike Mitchell's galloping steed! Something has changed in the vantage we have now on space and place and time.

It is this: even as Google continues the project of acquisitive traversal that capitalism and colonialism have impelled for centuries, it is doing something else too, perhaps inadvertently. The Street View/GIS nexus has brought the narrative hunger. Which is an unexpected affordance, I suggest, of the new technology. With the Google Car, the story that is meant to be ascribed to the journey is no longer obvious, no longer presumed and credited and credible, as it was when a sense of manifest destiny sustained the colonial venturers. With the zombie-affect of the stumbling, nine-eyed camera, no singular trajectory gets comfortably proposed. Instead of the colonialist narrative drive, instead of the modernist energy, we encounter diffused or 'ambient' perspectives and divergent throughlines.[18] The settings in Street View feel unfocused and 'agnostic' of destination. If you were to stitch traverser's tales into the scenes they would be plotted along several trajectories, out of several memories or toward many dissociated intrigues. The concussed and extensified journeys availed by Street View feel different from the rifling paths, so focused and intensified, that have already been scored by Mitchell and the *Mad Max* films. There is a feeling of blankness in the Googlescape, a manifest lack of narrative prescription. Encountering Street View, the traveller feels a strong yen to get involved with systems of stories. Ironically, the traveller yearns for something 'indigenous': a kind of orienting and all-encompassing story-network or mythology.

The yearning that you sense in Google's blankland is a hankering for 'country', a hunger for the system of place-tagged fabulations, dances, songs, painting, rituals and embodied memories that are kept and cosseted by the inhabitants (as distinct from the temporary travellers) in a storied domain. Country criss-crosses a terrain in all directions, narratively netting the meanings and emotions, the obligations and warnings that need to be acknowledged and retained as you find yourself and make your way through the place where you have landed, where you live. It is easy to invoke – this notion of country – but arduous to install and sustain, millennial in duration. True, it is a naïve and alarmingly rudimentary emotion, this parvenu hankering for country that one feels in the Street View blanklands. But there it is, calling for a new start.

With Street View, regarding the undead landscapes that the stumble-cam captures, they all have a vacuum in them. But they are strangely rousing nevertheless, no matter how meager, how depleted. I am reminded of Jay Leyda's brilliant insight that Emily Dickinson's utterances are so compelling because they have at their core an absence or silence where you would expect to hear divulgence, and in response to this 'omitted center' the reader floods feelings and notions into the exquisitely composed void.[19] Dickinson created this effect deliberately. With Google, I think, the structuring absence is accidental. But it is there nevertheless.

In summary, then, here is my thesis, offered with thanks to Kurgan and Barrell for lighting up Thomas Mitchell's journals and the *Mad Max* movies with fresh settings:

> There is an activating void in Google Street View which is an effect both of aesthetic qualities of the Google Camera's 360-degree pictorial field and of the mechanical triggering of the camera's automatic sequencing. The absence of meanings and feelings plus the lack of a singular perspectival impetus in the imagery stimulates in the viewer not only an urge to offer stories that account for the appearance of the scenes but also an urge to inhabit those scenes with human history.

Effectively, the wraparound landscapes of Street View spur viewers to append tales to the journeys via Google's pinning systems and via their own blogs and aggregation communities. Thus viewers can begin to participate in the narrative enrichment of the Googlescape's vacuous settings. More than being *receivers* of stored-up information, the viewers have the chance – singly and communally – to be *contributors* to the meanings and structures of feelings that give value to these landscapes which have been mapped as Google have compiled a kind of prospectus for future profitable uses of the traversed territories. Thus in their networked communality, these contributors have a chance to integrate a shared system of narratives which invest the traversed spaces with significance so that the most basic rudiments of a new kind of country-telling might start to take shape. Over time, as people offer their tales to fill the absences all over the Googlescapes, these contributors could become participants in country-keeping as they interact to make and maintain an ever-adjusting weave of plenteous, demotic narratives that hold information and emotion suffusing the entire, interconnected environment that hosts all the participant storytellers.

Immersed, and involved, not critically distanced, these country-keeping participants could make what James Agee once envisaged as a 'living map' that could be created through the prodigious testimonial work he craved in his account of Alabama in *Let Us Now Praise Famous Men*:

> let me hope the whole of that landscape we shall essay to travel in is visible and may be known as there all at once; let this be borne in mind, in order that, when we descend among its windings and blockades, into examination of slender particulars, this its wholeness and simultaneous living map may not be neglected, however lost the breadth of the country may be in the winding

walk of each sentence.[20]

To finish, resolving not to be stymied by the fact that this new, online mode of country-keeping is almost risibly inchoate at present, let's work a little harder with this idea of the *participant* in the living map. Let's see what can be done. With Google Street View, even as you serve the company by making data with your every action, you also become more than a participant; to a significant extent you are an *operator* of the viewing field, as you select the perspective and the trajectory of the Google Camera's journey. You attain a modicum of agency and responsibility. Operators are not readers or receivers. They can respond actively to the narrative hunger that presently aches in the Street View landscapes. Life in the Data Republic of Google is no Utopia. Indeed it feels increasingly like an oligarchy as well as a kind of political octopus, plainly, but there *is* something substantively fresh – for the moment at least – about the scenes that the company displays via its mapping systems.

In the Australian footprint of the Googleverse, we seem to be at a point of balance between plenitude and vacuity, a special point where the extensively measured and photographed environment is uncannily open for reimagining even as it is also being thoroughly itemized by the stocktaking of Google. For a myth can sometimes cause history to happen (as Ernst Cassirer so famously asserted) and a map can lead people back into country where no one has ventured in several generations.[21] So we have a chance to undercut, enrich and overlay the new acquisitive actions of Google and all the other data-miners. We can do this with fresh accounting, fresh narrating and fresh place-making in this our hyper-colonised sector of the dataverse. Curiously, unintentionally, we have been given a machine – this zombie-cam and its attendant satellites and networks – that might help us care for country in some new way, instead of just continuing to grab land in the old colonial way.

## Notes

1. Wislawa Szymborska (translated from the Polish by Clare Cavanagh), 'Map' in *The New Yorker*, 14 April 2014, pp. 46 – 7.
2. Laura Kurgan, *Close Up at a Distance: mappiung, technology, and politics*, Boston: MIT Press, 2013, p.14.
3. Kurgan, p. 14.
4. Kurgan, p. 16.
5. Kurgan, pp. 16–17.
6. Kurgan, p. 35.
7. Kurgan, p. 17.
8. Kurgan, p. 17.
9. Kurgan, p. 128.
10. David Shields *Reality Hunger: a manifesto*, New York: Knopf, 2010.
11. Three instances: Mishka Henner's 'No Man's Land' [http://www.mishkahenner.com/No-Man-s-Land]; Jon Rafman's '9 Eyes' which ponders the aesthetics and the seeming amorality of the 9-lensed surround-camera [http://9-eyes.com/]; my own 'Wayfaring Strangers' [rossgibson.com.au].
12. John Barrell, *The Dark Side of the Landscape: the rural poor in English painting 1730–1840*, Cambridge: Cambridge University Press, 1980; and John Barrell, *The Idea of Landscape and the Sense of Place 1730–1840; an approach to the poetry of John Clare*, Cambridge: Cambridge University Press, 1972.
13. Barrell, *The Idea of Landscape*, pp. 60–1
14. Barrell, *The Idea of Landscape*, pp. 62–3.
15. Michel Serres, with Bruno Latour, *Conversations on Science, Nature and Time* (translated by Roxanne Lapidus), Ann Arbor: The University of Michigan Press, 1995, p. 140.
16. Thomas Livingstone Mitchell, *Three Expeditions into the Interior of Eastern Australia*, 2 volumes, London: T. & W. Boone, 1838, vol. 1, p. 210.
17. Mitchell, *Three Expeditions*, vol. 1, p. 36.
18. Acknowledgements to Nikos Papastergiadis, in conversation, for this idea of 'ambient perspective'.
19. Jay Leyda, *The Years and Hours of Emily Dickinson*, North Haven (CT): Archon Press, 1970 (first published 1960, vol. 1, p.xxi.
20. James Agee, *Let Us Now Praise Famous Men*, first published 1941, reprinted London: Picador Classic, 1988, p.111.

21 See Ernst Cassirer, *The Philosophy of Symbolic Forms, Volume Two: mythical thought*, New Haven: Yale University Press, 1955, p. 5: 'In the relation between myth and history myth proves to be the primary, myth the secondary and derived, factor. It is not by its history that the mythology of a nation is determined but, conversely, its history is determined by its mythology – or rather the mythology of a people does not *determine* but *is* its fate, its destiny as decreed from the very beginning.'

# 9

# WAYFARING STRANGERS:
# ARTISTIC INVESTIGATIONS OF THE MOOD OF DARK TOURISM IN ONLINE MAPPING

On any leisured late night, preferably with a lamp lit against the somberness, you can search online for criminal court reports that will set you up for cruising via Google Street View to the photographed locations of the misdemeanours you've just probed. In digital Dallas (Texas), for example, you can convene your own motorcade, as millions have done, banking off Elm Street past the grassy knoll on Dealey Plaza.

Next from the shadow of the Book Depository you can drag the cursor way over the equator to a poverty-struck corner of South Australia, as dozens may have done. There you can trundle a route that starts at a site of horror in the body-dump bank vault on the main street of Snowtown and finishes in a somewhat hallucinatory aftermath out amidst the heart-stopping photogenics of the sea-coast along Myponie Point Drive, one hypnotic hour's travel from the gore.[1] (Full disclosure: I have driven through the Yorke Penisula a few times in the past and I recall eating a lunch comprised of a meat pie and a lemonade in a bakery in Snowtown sometime in the 1990s, albeit a full decade before the horrors of the bank vault. So I have an embodied memory of the place that Street View can rouse.) Even with your domestic comforts close by and with your computer-screen filtering the terror that once hit several poor souls unmediated, you will sense the isolation along Myponie and you might crave a status report from

Google: how many other folks are out here on this lonesome cybernetic road *right now* (which Google could tell you) and why are they abroad (which, most likely, not even the lurkers themselves could tell you).

Facilitated by Street View, these stakeouts make an odd and addictive kind of tourism. It is an experience steeped in the colonialism and globalisation that drives Google's mapping of space; it is an experience inviting reflection on how many ways you can be in space or move through it, how space can be something that you think you possess and utilise even as it holds and inhabits you. The Street View scenes hang between space and place, therefore; between land and landscape; between travel and tenure.

As mentioned in the previous chapter, John Barrell's great books *The Dark Side of the Landscape* and *The Idea of Landscape*, examine the rural politics and poetics in early-industrial England.[2] I will reprise here a brief portion of last chapter's argument again, in order set up the thesis about tourism that I want to propound now in this chapter.

As I have observed, Barrell details how land-tenure was transformed across most of Eighteenth-Century Britain so that extensive tracts that had long been held, farmed and husbanded communally, in a 'traditional' way, became intensive, enclosed estates that were owned personally, sequestered and exploited, in a 'modern' way. Barrell shows how the twinned phenomena of the Industrial Revolution and the Agricultural Revolution coincided in Britain not so much because farming was revamped by the invention and sudden availability of new machinery, as has been long surmised. Rather a change in *mentality* probably occurred first throughout the culture so that landgrabbing and the adoption of an entrepreneurial attitude to estates meant that the countryside came to be treated as an object full of raw materials and natural resources. In other words, the countryside was redefined as an agricultural object that could be processed with the efficiency-regimes afforded by the mechanical advantage and energy-transfer that were the drivers of the Industrial Revolution.[3]

As they acquired portfolios of estates, the new landed speculators became owners rather than tenders; no longer was it obvious that a person should come from and *belong to* one particular place. And someone who owns many places can quickly become accustomed to the idea that it is good to *move through* these places and to move from place to place as a celebration of personal sovereignty. These parvenu property-owners had found a modern, industrially efficient way to be in the space that they had managed to requisition, encompass and reap with movement that affords a kind of proprietorial ubiquity.

It was a simple next step to regard all land as matter waiting to be landscaped. In this process every representation of the countryside quickly appeared like a profiteer's prospectus, an offer to convert raw or natural resources to product and property. Unsurprisingly, tourism was not far behind this shift in mentality, with the exemplary vacation changing from the aristocratic gambit of the Grand Tour on the Continent to something more demotic, such that tourism became the popular pursuit of freedom, leisure and self-unfolding in other peoples' terrains. From early Victorian times onward, tourism became available to classes other than just the Ladies and Lords. Not only Counts' tours anymore, but Cooks Tours too.

Google Street View is the latest version of this tour across other peoples' terrains. In Australia, with Google's extensive photographic coverage of the continent's vastness, Street View affords a mode of travelling that feels like free and benign browsing, as if the intensively enclosed territories of the gridded world have been opened up and held in common again. This must be a good thing, all this liberty and self-direction, this easy permission to explore. Paradoxically though, the Street View experience also gives you a sense that digital travelling has a more malign mode. For despite the freedom to go mobile, digital travelling also offers a means of lurking and loitering. Invisibly, you can take the stance of a voyeuristic bystander, or an overseer, in scenes that are displayed in the aftermath of forensic recording. This sense of the aftermath is especially strong, of course, in Australia's colonial landscapes, where the country was seized not so long ago, most often violently.

When you go touring through Street View scenes, you can be visiting your own private manias; or to say it in a less sinister way, you can indulge your detective imagination. Clicking on the road ahead, lurching along forward, spinning now and then 360 degrees around, sometimes leaning back and up to ogle the vast witnessing skies that always bear down on the GoogleCar: the affect is lonesome and existential. For there is always this sense that something crucial is skulking behind you. It is like you are a sleuth re-opening a case that has gone cold. You can get the feeling you are one of those genre-narrative cops who cannot let their files rest, who have the grisliest pictures pinned on a wall in a motel room they have moved their clothes to. You go trudging through the screen to these aftermath scenes. You are anonymous in there but also vulnerable and exposed, paradoxically, even though there is usually no one to see and it feels like no one is seeing you.

At least, there is no one *obviously* seeing you. The paranoia in Street View tourism comes partly from knowing that you are making metadata, disturbing the scenes for higher-level investigators elsewhere. In other words, as you indulge your digital dark tourism, you get an irrational feeling that you are becoming a suspect. Someone is interested in your movements and motives. Someone you cannot identify or control. Indulging the freedom of the interface you feel a web of consequences wisp around you. This is a new version of the vortex of fate that elsewhere you have enjoyed watching film noir anti-heroes slide into. It amounts to nothing, most likely – this digital paranoia – but the unease can stay with you long after you have left the picture of the bank vault behind or clicked away from Myponie Point Drive. It starts out as a trip into curiosity and finishes in disorientation. You thought you were free to move, that the world was your bauble, but there is some other force roundabout you, more sovereign and extensive than yourself. As you stumble click-footed around Street View, it is rarely clear how many rights and responsibilities you have when lurking in the Google landscapes. Nor is it clear how many powerful forces are engaged around and behind your presence there, forces that are covert and difficult to negotiate. Unless you deliberately post up some images of your own when you are visiting, the traces that you leave in these scenes are perceptible only to the Google company, not to you or your fellow travellers.

Such is the tourist experience that I have sought to evoke and hold up for reflection in the ekphrastic compositions that I include in the second part of this essay. With these simple artworks I hope to give you some intensified access to the peculiar feeling of Street View dark tourism: how you feel free but obliged when cruising in Street View, how you are curious and without worries but wary also.

The ekphrastic compositions come from a film I have assembled from a thin line traced through the Googleverse, a film called 'Leaving Snowtown', which is part of a larger Street View project called 'Wayfaring Stranger'. The several components in 'Wayfaring Stranger' – films, fictional maps, light shows, paintings, textual and audio narratives, installation-environments and websites – arise from a set of research questions:

1. As I select particular images in Street View, I ask: how can I best show the viewer some vision that has in it an intensified understanding of the ways a digital traveller's freedom can be shadowed by dread?
2. Next, with the translations and manipulations that I bring to the original Google-snapped photographs, I ask: how can I best help the viewer understand the mood and hue of paranoia that often waits for the digital dark tourist?
3. Finally, with the words that I append to each image, I ask: how can I best make sense of the paradoxes of this image by offering an utterance that chimes for the viewer with some sense that is aesthetic and pre-cognitive, something extra to logic, something that intensifies the mood?

Let me explain this concern I have for mood. An encounter with a mood or an organised pattern of emotions is not usually the main quest for people visiting Google's vast panoply of mapped landscapes. Undeniably, however, these Street View images do have a stunned, machine-aesthetic that gives off a mood. And with varying degrees of conscious awareness, every visitor brings and stokes emotions that are served by this mood.

How to name this mood? The best way is to describe the emotions that well out of it. Curiosity so strong it becomes voyeurism: that is one of these emotions. Another tends to be disquiet. Uncanniness arises too.

Here is one reason I make these mood-soaked artworks: they let us visit a discomfiting emotion, via a mediated mood, *in a way that is safe because you can leave when you choose.* Horror movies are the classic example of this artistic licence. Similarly, online photographic mapping provides more than just an 'information environment'. More than just data and meanings, there are structures of feeling arrayed along and off to the side of the highways and byways of every Street View landscape.

But can you leave so blithely whenever you choose? In the Permissions FAQ pages of Google's website, there is a befuddling – actually it is disquieting – run of instructions and prohibitions that purport to be permissions. Here are just two snippets:

**Q: I'd like to use your maps in my project. What's the first thing I should know?**

**A:** To determine if your proposed use of Content is acceptable, you should first read closely the applicable Terms of Service:

Google Maps/Google Earth Terms and Conditions
Google Maps/Google Earth APIs Terms of Service

Your use of Content, as defined in the Terms of Service, in anything from marketing and promotional materials to films and books is first and foremost governed by the license provided in the applicable Terms of Service for the product. In certain circumstances, Google may be able to grant you a broader license to use the Content in a manner not covered in the Terms of Service. Plus, apart from any license granted to you by Google, your use of Content may be acceptable under principles of "fair use."

Fair use is a concept under copyright law in the U.S. that, generally speaking, permits you to use a copyrighted work in certain ways without obtaining a license from the copyright holder. There are a variety of factors that affect whether your use of Content would be considered fair use, including the purpose and character of your use, the nature of the copyrighted work, the amount of the copyrighted material used, and the effect of your use upon the potential market for the copyrighted work. For example, there are differences between use in a for-fee service and use in a work of scholarship, or the use of a single map screenshot and the use of detailed map images for an entire country. There are similar, although generally more limited, concepts in other countries' copyright laws, including a concept known as "fair dealing" in a number of countries. That all being said...

**Please do not request that we interpret whether your use of Content is fair use.** Google cannot tell you if your use of Content from our products would be fair use or would be considered fair dealing; these are legal analyses that depend on all of the specific facts of your proposed use. We suggest you speak with an attorney if you have questions regarding fair use of copyrighted works.

Q: May I alter your imagery for my project?

A: Any use of Google Maps and Google Earth must reflect how the products and imagery would look online. For example, you are not allowed to make any changes (e.g. delete, blur, etc.) to our products or imagery that would make these items look genuinely different. This includes, but is not limited to, adding clouds or other natural elements, altered user-interfaces, and modifications that do not appear in the actual product. However, Google offers a Styled Maps

> API which allows you to edit the colors of individual map components as well as toggle visibility for each component (i.e. change water to purple and make roads invisible).

It is actually unclear how legally unencumbered even this very moment of quoting has been. For I have clipped this text directly from Google's website as two substantial onscreen images, using them holus-bolus for my own purposes. Have I stolen and exploited Google property for my project? It is obviously an academic use and there is no way I will make one half of a red cent from the action. So, academic comment, fair-review provisions and the plain avoidance of commercial exploitation all customarily cover such uses and I would not expect any cavilling from a publisher or the rights-holder.

But in the digital subsets of IP law, all that was relatively solid is still up in the air. So here is the paranoid vortex at work: first you have a harmless, innocent thought; next you feel the dread when you act on it. As Google asserts its rights over its images – which is close to asserting rights over the imagistic understanding of places that other people have long constructed and cared for – the company deliberately produces ambiguities which serve to emphasise its power even as it remains ambiguous about its benevolence. This is the company, remember, whose mission was often declared in the early days to be the avoidance of evil. No simple statement, that one, when the ownership of images of other peoples' habitats and range-lands is involved.

So I have been investigating these conundrums of freedom and entrapment via a series of artworks, of which 'Leaving Snowtown' (excerpted below) is a small component. Resolving to accentuate the ambiguities of Street View tourism – its attractions and repulsions, its ease and its disquiet – I have developed the work as follows:

> First, I selected one image each for three particularly 'resonant' scenes in and around Snowtown, scenes with *aesthetic* qualities that gave off for me some special feeling that has helped me consider afresh the awful power of events that took place there.
> Next I noted the URL of each of these images.
> Then I emailed that line of code to China, to a service that promises to turn any image into 'an art painting' – your choice of ink, watercolour, acrylics or oils – which they promise to post to you express.

There was one more factor: when I sent the URL I requested an extra phase of translation. I had noticed that the painting service invites clients to append notes to the job-sheet, whereby you can suggest a stylistic approach you would like them to try. So I asked if my picture could be given a 'Giorgio Morandi feeling'. I sent them a sample image of one of the Bolognese master's muted landscapes (rarer but no less poignant than his *natura morta*) and I suggested that the best medium would be watercolour.

After a few weeks my Chinese package arrived. Now I had some anonymous piece-worker's translations of my selected images, which were already translations of my memories of having visited the town, memories that were all filtered now through the provocations offered by the Google-camera and the digital encoding and compositing effects that are inherent to the jpeg format. The pictures had something weirder and better than charm in them, but they were not yet generating the sense of hazed concussion and repercussion that I thought the original locations exuded. So I scanned the watercolours and made them into fresh digital files. Then I worked on them some more in Photoshop, choosing at last the 'Box Blur' filter to render these much-mutated crime scene images into some kind of stun-dreamed abstraction of what my younger self (when I visited Snowtown some time in the 1990s) and then later the automatic Google Camera had witnessed. My hope is that 'mood' more than 'information' is what now shines through so that the Street View mapping system has become a portal not only to interpretive intellection but also to a kind of emotional divination.

As the last stage of the process, having fixed the right quality of the image, I added two breath-short utterances to each picture, utterances that drop the viewer into a fragment of a narrative that galvanises the scene, utterances that might grant the viewer some concentrated, forensic insight into the dark tourist unease that waits in these locations – actual and virtual.

The aim of 'Leaving Snowtown' (and of the entire 'Wayfaring Stranger' suite) is to concoct in the viewer an enhanced understanding of the structured feelings that can be mapped across places. Together the image and text are designed to intensify, by aesthetic and evocative means rather than with direct explanation, the viewer's sense of how it *feels* to be a tourist 'out here' in the dark non-space of cybernetics, where photographic representations of real worlds are observed, moved and consumed in fibre-optic shimmers. The aim is to help us know better the paradox of Street View's digital tourism: to know how we are free to come, lurk and go while we are also entangled by every move that we make in a real world that is both geographic and ghosted by captured information concerning our actions; to know how we make our own aftermaths there.

'Leaving Snowtown'

Witness what's been waiting here.
Leave the town all comatose.

*Photoshop 'Box Blur' abstraction of a Chinese watercolour of an onscreen image of the bank in Snowtown.*

Go faster than your wheels allow.
Roll back to a canted ditch.

*Photoshop 'Box Blur' abstraction of a Chinese watercolour of an onscreen image of a dirt road at the municipal limits of Snowtown.*

Steep down in the estuary reach.
Let landscape take your supine form.

*Photoshop 'Box Blur' abstraction of a Chinese watercolour of an onscreen image of a seaside dirt track known as Myponie Point Drive in the Yorke Peninsula, one hour out of Snowtown.*

## Notes

1  Search Google for 'Snowtown murders'.
2  John Barrell, *The Dark Side of the Landscape: the rural poor in English painting 1730–1840,* Cambridge: Cambridge University Press, 1980; and John Barrell, *The Idea of Landscape and the Sense of Place 1730–1840; an approach to the poetry of John Clare,* Cambridge: Cambridge University Press, 1972.
3  See Barrell, *The Idea of Landscape,* pp. 60–1.

# 10

## GHOSTS OF A BETTER TOMORROW: THE VOLATILE FORMALISM OF 1980S FILM WORKSHOP PRODUCTIONS IN HONG KONG

Does anyone recall *The Exploded Form* (1980), James Mellard's pithy book about modernist aesthetics? Surprising, how it isn't more widely cited. The main thesis is as bold as it is simple: granted, says Mellard, modernism is customarily portrayed as a set of distortions and cerebral attacks on commonsense worldviews; however, despite all its apparently 'unnatural' distortions of form – think of literary vorticism or of painterly cubism – modernism should be understood as directly *mimetic* of lived experience, not at odds with it. In other words, modernism is best regarded as high-fidelity realism. Not a disorienting attack on the detailed naturalism that produced Zola's descriptive novels, let's say. Not a mind-bending assault on the ocular normality obeyed in the impressionists' attentiveness to the scintillations of Parisian sunshine. No, modernism commenced as an exercise in realistic, contemporary exactitude. It was an attempt to render in aesthetic form the real perceptual and emotional shocks that slammed into the sensorium of any twentieth-century European person, every moment of every day.

Modernism was produced for and by a generation who experienced the literal explosions of World War One and for metropolitan artists trying to assimilate to the paroxysmic shifts of informatic and physical speed in the electrified cities of the early twentieth century. The modernist ploys that have often been summarized glibly as 'formalist experiments' or 'defamiliarisation routines' showed how space and time really do get convulsed by a mortar shell, for example, or really do warp and splinter when you hurtle through a metropolitan business district on a trolley car. The absence of a single, fixed perspective-point; the mixing of top into bottom, left into right, exterior into interior; the dismembering of bodies and heretofore familiar objects and places: for Mellard, all these purportedly 'shocking', 'illogical' motifs can be regarded as straightforward presentations of everyday life.

Mellard's thesis always comes to mind – or more exactly, I always feel its truth in my nervous system – when I go back and watch Hong Kong cinema from the 1980s, particularly the early Film Workshop 'classics' produced by Tsui Hark. It's not Mellard's definition of *modernism*, exactly, that appeals to me when I look back; rather it's his idea that aesthetic forms are *really* shaped to the quotidian experiences prevailing at the time of their creation. For me, films such as the *Chinese Ghost Story* series and the *Better Tomorrow* trilogy were stamped by Hong Kong's nervous reality during the decade before the 1997 'handover' to the mainland Chinese government. Consider the kinetic, elastic formalism of the *Chinese Ghost Story* films, a formalism that remakes space and time in such a way that it usually gets tagged perfunctorily as 'fantastic'. Consider how there are actual, embodied concerns given explicit, *palpable* form in these films: namely, rootlessness, fearfulness and the necessity to invent mercurial configurations of self, place and community in circumstances that are always insecure and shifting. As Grady Hendrix has explained the set-up, it's a formal patterning shaped for a changeful society full of recent arrivals and provisional inhabitants:

> [migrants] know the bitter taste of premature partings and the absurdity of keeping a place in their hearts for a homeland they barely remember. They know that borders make all the difference and that citizenship is destiny: a chemical engineer in Bombay is a cab driver in New York; a screw-up in London is a bank manager in Hong Kong. ... Tsui's characters are neither here nor there, subject to sudden, traumatic changes in status and identity.[1]

In this chapter, I want to hold the idea of migrant restlessness in the foreground so we consider how a brief moment of formalist cinema history conjoined with a moment of populist nationalism in Hong Kong during the 1980s. I'd like to learn something from the sensations I get when reviewing the early years (1987–89) of Film Workshop, not long after the company really made its mark with the exhilarating *Peking Opera Blues* in 1986.

First though, in order to see more clearly the significance of these selected years, we need a quick cultural history, to get the context in which the *Ghost Stories* and the *Better Tomorrows* burst into Hong Kong history and into cinema history.

★ ★ ★

Most chronicles of Hong Kong recognise that as far as sovereignty goes, the island is up for grabs. It always has been. And while no historian can seriously press a British claim anymore, the question of native title – of originary, authentic 'Hong Kong-ness' – still seems unanswerable. As G. B. Endacott suggests in his standard *History of Hong Kong*, an indigenous populace is not clearly recognisable in recorded history.² Since the fifteenth century there have been two main designations of 'Hong Kong person': there are the folk called *poon tei*, which is a Cantonese word for 'local'; and there have been the slightly less local folk called *hakka*, a word which has multiple meanings but can be translated as 'guest people'. Then there are the expats. In other words, in Hong Kong one might expect to find Chinese people born on or near the island, plus people from the broader Cantonese environs, plus unspecified aliens from farther afield who are temporarily resident for sundry reasons. Some of these latter might be Chinese, some might be only somewhat Chinese and some will be definitely not Chinese. But no matter where they or their ancestors might have hailed from, everyone in all the above categories will be HongKongese somehow.

Assessed over the millennial spans of time that usually define indigeneity, Hong Kong is home to no singular culture or ethnicity. This is especially true when one remembers that 'China' is a plural concept covering a profusion of languages and histories. Over the past six hundred years, Hong Kong island has harboured an ever-mutating agglomeration of gleaners, pirates, runaways, bivouacing fishing fleets, merchants, market gardeners, profiteers, traders, artisans and homemakers. From the outset it has been a culture of displacement, flux and negotiation.

Then at the end of the seventeenth century, everything intensified when European traders gathered in great numbers around Canton. Thus the island in the deep outer wash of the Pearl River watersheds became a crucial harbor granting access to the massive province now known as Guangdong. Services developed for the thronging trading vessels, and a scrappy market of dispute and haggle began to grow into an economy of unprecedented, international scale.

The European trade systems brought their customary competition and conflict, which climaxed in the 'opium wars' of 1840, whereby Britain seized control of the island. In 1843 the British government declared Hong Kong a colony of the Crown. And the population and architecture of the place started to grow, fester-fashion. During the remainder of the nineteenth century a transient population of small-traders, garden-farmers, fisher folk and labourers – dubbed 'the scum of Canton' by disgruntled British colonial administrators – formed the majority of the Hong Kong population. (Indeed, in 1843, the wastrel taint ascribed to the island prompted a British plan, which was never implemented, to clean up the Hong Kong population by transporting local 'wrongdoers' to New South Wales.)

So although contemporary Hong Kong is one of the most sophisticated and legalised jurisdictions on earth, a readiness to indulge in quicksilver profiteering is its birthright. And rootlessness is its continuing elan. Not for Hong Kong, the myths of groundedness and generational custodianship that are basic to most national identities. Hong Kong's myths – if its cinema is anything to go by – tell of wrenching displacement, mutability and a savvy kind of entrepreneurial energy always on the make.

Certainly the history of *cinema* in Hong Kong is a story of relentless change, transplantation and hustle, to the extent that the adaptive redeployment of a clutch of *poon tei* story-systems has itself become a robust Hong Kong tradition as filmmakers exploit whatever is available (street-theatre and folktales included) to help them respond to the squalls of political and economic change that constantly buffeted the region.

Speaking of changefulness, 1937 was a crucial year in Chinese cinema. The Japanese stormed Shanghai, virtually shutting down Chinese film production. Shanghai filmworkers fled in several directions, depending on their political affiliations. Many joined Chiang Kai-Shek's Nationalist government upriver in Wuhan and Chongqing; some fled to the Communists in Yan'an; some lay low in the foreign municipalities that persisted in Shanghai; others took cover from the coming mainland conflagration by fleeing to different kinds of risks in Hong Kong. Film production in all destinations was severely curtailed for the next ten years, firstly by the Sino-Japanese conflict, then by World War II and the ensuing power struggle between the Communists and the Nationalists.

By 1947, therefore, history had spawned three radically different Chinese film industries. Communist-backed studios were commencing work in Shanghai and Xingshan; Nationalist loyalists, predominantly documentarists, retreated to Taiwan; and filmmakers in Hong Kong found themselves affiliated to a strange new pan-Asian and transnational rule of commerce. This was vassalage of its own kind, of course, but it did free up Hong Kong filmmakers to try out styles and genres that either had not yet been perfected or had been outlawed since the 1930s. An example of the latter was the martial-arts genre known in the critical parlance of the 1950s as 'fantastique style'. Banned by the Nationalists in the 1930s because of its blithe rambunctiousness and its disregard of most laws (including Newtonian physics), this genre entwining ectoplasmic energy-flow and magic into swordplay, weightless combat and fiendish chicanery came back strongly in Hong Kong. Drawing many of their personnel from the schools of Peking Opera that were being established in Hong Kong, these films were displays of gymnastic, choreographic and montagist virtuosity. Not so much narrative as *performative*, the films were packages of outbursting energy sprung endlessly with rapid-response ingenuity. They were the cinematic strain of the martial arts romances that had flourished in market theatres, city operas and village storytelling for centuries.³

The 'fantastique' films found their audiences (*poon tei* and *hakka*) and during the 1950s the genre boomed as markets also expanded in Singapore, Malaysia and to a lesser degree, in Viet nam and the United States. The kinetic style evolved further during the 1960s, taking guttural stylistic flourishes from Japanese samurai epics, 'chambara' movies and TV serials. (Chambara is an onomatopoeic word for the noise of clashing swords.) But as they absorbed new influences, the films remained markedly 'HongKongese' in character. As Geoffrey O'Brien has emphasised, 'whatever stylistic devices the Hong Kong film makers may have appropriated, the tone of their films remained entirely different from the Japanese, eschewing the strain of pessimism ... which informs [post-WWII Japanese] movies like *Lightning Swords of Death* or *Trail of Blood*'.⁴

Boisterous as they were, the Hong Kong films presented a kind of febrile optimism upheld against uncertainty. Thus the way was being laid for the emergence of the *kung fu* movies that commanded great attention during Bruce Lee's short, dazzling career. The Lee films still show today how an arresting dexterity and an uplifting grace can temper histrionic cruelty. The Lee films arose out of a by-then vibrant tradition of Hong Kong cinema and Asian migrant savvy, a persistent celebration of the cerebral and bodily wit of the trickster, the performer, the adaptive character who refuses to be overwhelmed by the stupidities of established authority. As *Fists of Fury* and *Way of the Dragon* testify, kung fu cinema can activate a choreographic beauty that has so much resourceful brute-force that it feels like a life-force.

By the 1970s, therefore, the 1950s 'fantastique' format had altered, but it was definitely in rude health and was available to a new generation of filmmakers who had travelled and studied widely and were ready to supplement existing styles and genres with techniques, attitudes and storylines looted freely from world cinema. After Bruce Lee's death in 1973, when the major studios (in the USA as well as Hong Kong) were casting around for a replacement star or a replacement star-genre, the scene was set for a turbulent decade when a new bunch of producers and directors might seize the initiative in Hong Kong. It was in these circumstances that, most famously, Tsui Hark and Nansun Shi's Film Workshop and Jacky Chan and Samo Hung's productions for the mega-studio Golden Harvest became so popular in the local scene.

These are by no means the only major players in the late-twentieth-century history of an industry which, during the 1980s, produced well in excess of one hundred officially-registered feature films annually. But as a way of seeing into some peculiarities of Hong Kong and its film industry right up to the present-day, the early years of Film Workshop offer a good starting point, not least because the company was responsible for some of the most exhilarating and shrewd movies ever made, but also because the studio's work has already attracted a good array of critical description and analysis in English-language journals and fanzines.

Film Workshop was formed in 1984 by director/producer Tsui Hark and producer Nansun Shi. Tsui had recently completed the hits *Aces Go Places III* and *Zu, Warrior of Magic Mountain* for Golden Harvest and he was therefore one of the most bankable directors in Hong Kong. Hustling extra investment on the strength of this celebrity, Film Workshop set up a special effects research and production unit, called Cinefex Workshop, which was to develop techniques and technologies for booting the 'fantastique' genre into a new phase. The fortunes of the new company were well assured by the success of their debut film *Shanghai Blues* in

1985 and by the record returns from the gangster film, *A Better Tomorrow* directed by John Woo and produced by Tsui in 1986. Then the benefits of Cinefex became obvious in 1987 when the first *Chinese Ghost Story* appeared, directed with myriad 'impossible' moves by Ching Siu tung. Film Workshop arrived and became definitive very quickly.

Surviving right up to the present day, the company has made more than eighty features in a profusion of genres, including a bold push into big-budget animation and television series, while riding through a couple of boom-and-bust cycles in China plus an underwhelming attempt by Tsui and John Woo to storm the Hollywood system. All the time, right across the array of productions, one can discern a few fundamental consistencies in form, characterisation and theme in their projects. Regardless of whether they are set in the past, present or future, Film Workshop movies conjure almost always a shapeshifting prize called 'China', a dynamically modelled world of desire and potentiality which is not stable like something readily habitable but which can be experienced momentarily as an intensity of wishing and imagining, like a dream you can't relinquish even in your waking hours. It is the *feeling* generated in the films that compels the viewer, not the thesis. And every time, the feeling that stays with the viewer is *vitality*.

Film Workshop projects are typically set in circumstances of extreme mutability, jazzed with a sense of limitless possibility. Certainly this is the case in the three *Ghost Story* films (all directed by Ching Siu Tung) and the three *Better Tomorrows* (the first two of which were directed by Woo, the third by Tsui). In fact this vitality – scrambled as it always is with a bamboozling volatilty – is a characteristic taken from the chivalric romances which have been so influential in Cantonese cinema. These folktales are usually set in the *jiang-hu* (the 'vagrant world'), a fabled place-and-time 'without rules', a society that's always being assailed (or enlivened) by a rabble of renegades, speech-makers, martial artists, wandering scholars, ghosts and mountebanks. The *jiang-hu* provides a setting with evocative parallels to contemporary Hong Kong, where everyone has to negotiate the uncertainty of their twinned vassalage to transnational capitalism and Chinese New Communism. So it is not surprising that Tsui Hark plays so many variations on the vagrant-world theme. It has been *the* theme for the past fifty years or more in Hong Kong – in cultural artefacts and in everyday life.

Moreover Tsui's own biography is a relatively benign version of a *jiang-hu* tale. The story he usually puts about is that he grew up as an alien Chinese in Vietnam before moving to Hong Kong as a teenager and then travelling to study in Texas. He worked in community television and newspapers in New York City's Chinatown before returning to Hong Kong in the late 1970s to direct a popular television serial. His early feature film career took him to Taiwan at one stage and his later career has taken him to Los Angeles, but he continues to make his home in Hong Kong, 'home' being a definitively slippery notion, of course.

All the *Ghost Story* films and the *Better Tomorrows* are set in peculiar variants of the *jiang-hu*, in belief-systems, times and spatial environments defined by maximal flux. The *Ghost Stories*, for example, occur in an unspecified past ransacked by self-serving marketeers, eternity-suspended ghosts, loutish police, destitute scholars, reclusive Taoists and insurgent faux-Buddhists. More contemporary, but no less fabulist, the *Better Tomorrow* films take place in a world that is both created and annihilated by a shifty brotherhood of a panAsian criminal caste, a world where characters search for a reliable value – call it loyalty, love or peace – on which to base plans for a life that might, just possibly, survive into a future that's free from dread and deceit. In the gangster *jiang-hu*, friends become enemies in the wink of an eye; undercover cops reach for the riches of the criminals they are meant to be ghosting; criminals yearn for a time when they will be allowed to live righteously. Moreover, the ascension to power provides nothing like control or stability: the air-conditioned office of the successful gangster is as treacherous and restless a place as a haunted temple; and the city outside is a space of extreme unreliability and disorientation. (As an epigraph to Tsui's *Butterfly Murders* [1979] puts it, 'Be it the rich, be it the poor, they have become bleached bones all the same. And who can speak of victory?')

Made and set well before the 1997 handover of British Hong Kong to Communist China, the two trilogies comprise a paradoxically jubilant and boisterous *jiang-hu* for the future, a time which will require political dispassion interlaced with personal compassion, plus ethical ingenuity jazzed with prodigious physical and psychic energy.

In all six films, historical time is presented as a hydra-headed thing which fragments and proliferates as you examine it. Or more precisely, there is no one system of time: each character inhabits and activates a flurry of time scales and events, all inter-related but individual. The films, like Hong Kong itself, are assemblages of characters, locales and temporal rhythms all trying out new ways to cohere.

Sometimes housing, sometimes hindering the ever-warping timescales and generational *dramatis personae* of all six films, there are the fabulously unconstrained spaces. Repeatedly throughout each film, the viewer feels a giddy sense of 'impossible' placement and imminent re-location while watching the characters fight, fly, disappear, re-emerge and strive to be everywhere and nowhere all at once in locales that refuse to remain static. The experience is analogous to being a citizen of a state that is endlessly leased, leached and traded by larger, incursive forces. And to the extent that utopia is 'no-place', Film Workshop creates a pantopia where all spatio-temporal realignments show themselves to be possible, for good and for bad.

Undeniably, there is exhilaration as well as disorientation in the *Ghost Stories* and the *Better Tomorrows*. For the viewers as well as the protagonists, the normlessness delivers not a paralysis but a profusion of options. In the decade before the 1997 handover, the Film Workshop movies refused to be merely melancholy, elegiac or tragic. Rather, they offered intensified feelings of vaulting transcendence in response to the challenges and opportunities of rootlessness and future uncertainty. This is why the tradition of 'fantastique style' was so avidly inherited and modified by Film Workshop. As the films presented their protean spaces, rhythms and manoeuvres, they induced a neurological joy in the viewer, a tingling, truly felt 'affect' of triumph in response to impediment and mortality. Formally, the films were shaped to the exigencies of their time and place. Their aesthetic form was mimetic of both the realpolitik and the real emotional turbulence in peoples' everyday life in that place at the time. It is in this respect that James Mellard's 'exploded form' thesis feels so right. *Fantastique* as the Film Workshop productions are, they are also *realist*.

Summing up the impact of the early Film Workshop productions, therefore, it is valid to think back through their narrative patterns, looking for meanings or messages; but it is even more germane to monitor how you are *feeling* as you are being moved all over the films' temporal and spatial settings. Like a good video game, the narratives in these films are mostly frameworks for regimes of synaptic rhythm and cardio-vascular patterns of dread-versus-hope, fight-versus-flight, tension-versus-release that all interlace to induce paroxysms and relaxations which may not be readily translated into the conventional semantics of film theory but which are vehemently significant nevertheless. To quote Geoffrey O'Brien again, the 1980s Film Workshop movies are 'presentational' rather than 'representational'.[5] They have force more than meaning; they move the viewer because of what they do rather than what they refer to or what interpretations they induce. Thus their form mimics the real conditions of yearning and dreading that galvanised the society in which they were produced.

And what these films do, by the time the credits roll and put a temporary end to all the anti-gravity and time-scrunching, is buoy up the affections of a community of viewers who are potentially weighed down by uncertainty. In a place ghosted by all the disempowerments in its past and bolstered by no guarantees of a better tomorrow, these films don't tell their audiences how to find sanctuary, but they do offer palpable versions, right now, of how such unfettered sovereignty might feel in your own skin, in your nerves and bones.

## Notes

1. Grady Hendrix, 'Tsui Hark', *Senses of Cinema*, an online journal http://www.sensesofcinema.com/contents/directors/03/tsui.html
2. G.B. Endacott, *A History of Hong Kong*, London: Oxford University Press, 1958, p. 3, and following
3. Refer to Lin Nien-tung, 'The Martial Arts Hero', in Leong Mo-ling (ed.), *A Study of the Hong Kong Swordplay Film*, Fifth Hong Kong International Film Festival, 1981. See also Yu Mo-wan, 'Swords, Chivalry and Palm Power: a brief survey of the Cantonese martial arts cinema', in Leong Mo-ling (ed.), *A Study of the Hong Kong Swordplay Film*, Fifth Hong Kong International Film Festival, 1981.
4. Geoffrey O'Brien, 'Blazing Passions', *The New York Review of Books*, September 1992, p. 40.
5. Geoffrey O'Brien, 'Blazing Passions', p. 41.

## FURTHER READING

Armanet, Francois and Max, *Cine Kung Fu*, Paris: Editions Ramsay, 1988.

Berry, Chris (ed.), *Perspectives on Chinese Cinema*, London: BFI, 1991.

Berry, Chris, 'Heterogeneity as Identity: hybridity and transnationality as foundation myths in Hong Kong and Yaiwan cinema', in *METRO: The Media Magazine*, 91(Spring 1992), pp. 48–51.

Bordwell, David, *Planet Hong Kong: popular cinema and the art of entertainment*, Cambridge, MA: Harvard University Press, 2000.

Dannen, Fredric and Long, *Hong Kong Babylon: the insider's guide to the Hollywood of the East*, New York: Miramax, 1997.

Fonoroff, Paul, 'A Brief History of Hong Kong Cinema', in *Renditions: a Chinese-English translation magazine,* vol. 29–30 (Spring-Autumn 1988), pp. 293–308.

Gu Long, *On Wu Xia: one of the seven weapons – the sword of immortality*, Taiwan: Han Lin Publishing, 1978.

Hampton, Howard. 'Once Upon a Time in Hong Kong: Tsui Hark and Ching Siu-tung.' *Film Comment*, July-August 1997.

Hutchings, Peter, 'From the Wicked City', in *Filmnews*, July 1993, pp. 8–10.

Liu, James, *The Chinese Knight-Errant*, Chicago: University of Chicago Press, 1967.

Lent, John, *The Asian Film Industry*, Austin: University of Texas Press, 1990.

Leong Mo-ling (ed.) *A Study of the Hong Kong Swordplay Film*, The Fifth Hong Kong International Film Festival, 1981.

Nery, Robert, 'Hong Kong Fireworks', in *Filmnews*, May 1991.

Pattison, Barrie, 'Tsui Hark', in *Fatal Visions*, 12 (April 1992) and 13 (October 1992).

Rayns, Tony, 'Hard Boiled', in *Sight and Sound*, August 1992.

Teo, Stephen, *Hong Kong Cinema: the extra dimensions*, London: British Film Institute, 1997.

Wark, McKenzie, 'Disseminating Cinema: in praise of Hong Kong movies', in *Filmviews*, Summer 1987–88.

Yang, Jeff, Gan, Hong, *Eastern Standard Time: a guide to Asian influence on American culture*. Boston: Houghton Mifflin, 1997.

**See also** the special issue of *Cahiers du cinema* (September 1984) on Hong Kong cinema.

**See also** the back issues of *Cinemaya*.

## 11

## CAST AGAINST TYPE

In January 1788 Lieutenant William Dawes landed in Sydney Cove as part of the task force implementing the colonial experiment that has become modern Australia. Dawes was a man fixed within frames. He was a surveyor and cartographer intent on viewing and gridding land through Euclidian formats and arithmetical layouts. Precocious, the twenty-six-year-old had several other vocations. Extra to his mapping roles, he was an engineer who constructed the armatures of battlements and the edifices of bridges and observatories for the new colony. He was also an astronomer who focused his vision through sextants and scopes and methodised his thinking in columns of trigonometrical calculus designed to bring regularity to the starburst of details that outreached peripheral vision and European knowledge of the austral heavens. In fact, the reason Dawes was in the First Fleet was because the Astronomer Royal, Nevil Maskelyne, the close protégé of the King of England, had insisted that the bright young man be employed to pursue the lofty sciences in the South Land. Contrarily though, the colonial Governor Arthur Phillip only valued Dawes for his concrete skills, for his surveying and road-building.

Mostly self-taught, Dawes had a genius for pattern-seeking and for understanding systems – numerical, sonic, relational systems. For example he was the first person to listen intensively and extensively in order to figure how to write down an Australian language. In two precious notebooks – fewer than one hundred pages of handwriting – he listed nouns and verbs and he gave accounts of vignettes and clipped scenarios rendered in bilingual narration. He was a list-maker but also a storyteller therefore. Here we see him as a paradox, in this interplay between the fixed arraignments in his tabulations and the flowing melodics and delineations and fugitive divagations of his narration. We see him to be a man of frames but also a man out of bounds.

And we can see that he is not simply admirable. For one thing, despite all of his apparent sensitivity to Indigenous mentalities, he was undeniably a military man, a marine lieutenant in the squadron that seized the country of the canoe-navigating Sydney Harbour people (who are generally known as the Gadigal) and the pedestrian hinterland people (who are generally known as the Duarag). He was a paradox this way.

Having studied Dawes for twenty years, I've come to see him as an attractive monster. He was a monster in the original sense of the word: a kind of freak that turns up and shows us something, as in 'demonstrates'. And he was monster in the way he brought a warning, as in 'admonition'. He brought a warning about the loss of something remarkable: a consciousness exquisitely attuned to the dynamics of the Australian part of the world. Also he was a monster in the contemporary sense of the word: he had some repellent qualities. But he was brilliant and attractive too. No one character-type pins him down. With his paradoxical qualities, Dawes can help us grasp a period of befuddlement in global history and in the composition of individual Western psychology. For he lived through a period of change in social systems, change in philosophical configurations of the world, and he knew change in the ways a European individual's persona might be conceived or construed.

Which brings us to the offer of this chapter: I have no rights or intentions to explain Sydney Aboriginal culture in depth, but I can wonder out loud about the blurs and edges of character-types that get highlighted when we assay the paradox of William Dawes when he was interacting with the Sydney people. Through him we might ask some telling questions about the self, society and sense-making and we might see into the extraordinary heterogeneity of personality types that he performed during his time at Sydney Cove, when so many contradictions disallowed a simple, universal understanding of human values and obligations.

So … we have already learned that we can know Dawes *somewhat* with reference to the range of his vocational types: he was a cartographer, surveyor, engineer, astronomer, military man, a man capable of doing the regulated, coordinated, disciplined work which brings a profusion of information into some particular, methodical order which can stand as knowledge. Furthermore, being an assiduous notetaker and listmaker – with his survey charts, his almanacs and astronomical ledgers, his language notebooks – Dawes was a man of the page, literally a man defined by type.

The page is perhaps the most demanding and productive of framing and character-ascribing systems. What is it to write? What is it to read? What is it to expect that relationship through the page between a writer and a reader, through the page and through time between a writer in the eighteenth century, let's say, and a reader in the twenty-first century?

The classicist Anne Carson analyses the affordances of the inscribed page vividly, pondering how the pressures on human consciousness work differently in oral and written cultures:

> The difference revolves around the physiological and psychological phenomenon of individual self-control. Self-control is minimally stressed in an oral milieu where most of the data important for survival and understanding are channeled into the individual through the open conduits of his senses, particularly his sense of sound, in a continuous interaction linking him with the world outside him.[1]

This shift from oral to written is not necessarily an evolutionary advance. It is just a shift in cognitive mode, a shift in the ways a person can be in and of the world, in correspondence with the world full of others. Individuality contends with communality. The fixity of self versus the dispersion of self into communality. There are gains and losses, benefits and deficits in the predominance of each mode: the written versus the oral. Carson elaborates:

> Complete openness to the environment is a condition of optimum awareness and alertness for such a person [in an oral milieu], and a continual fluent interchange of sensual impressions and responses between the environment and himself is the proper condition of his physical and mental life. To close his senses off from the outside world would be counterproductive to life and to thought.[2]

Carson is referring explicitly to the transition from oral to written modes within Ancient Greek culture. But her ideas help us think about what must have been felt when Dawes brought the written mode of language to the Sydney people. The existential change, by which I mean the adjustment to the sense of environmental connectedness and interpersonal obligation portended in this new practice, was profound:

> Reading and writing require focusing the mental attention upon a text by means of the visual sense. As an individual reads and writes he gradually learns to close or inhibit the input of his senses, to inhibit or control the responses of his body, so as to train energy and thought upon the written words. He resists the environment outside him by distinguishing and controlling the one inside him. … In making the effort he becomes aware of the interior self as an entity separable from the environment and its input[,] controllable by his own mental action … the individual personality gathers itself to resist disintegration.[3]

In the interaction between a reader and the printed page, the self becomes a kind of calibrated engine applied to a settled and set-aside world of raw significance that awaits the formative actions of an author.

And what of the qualities of words, precisely? How do words mutate when speech ceases being an airy event where language is the utterance of breath pulsing in a continuous world of sound and changes to a technologised scene where words are clipped things fixed visibly on a page?

Carson provides an answer by focusing on edges and frames:

> [Once they are printed on a surface] … words have edges. Heard words may have no edges, or varying edges; oral traditions may have no concept of 'word' as a fixed and bounded vocable. Homer's word for 'word'

(*epos*) includes the meanings 'speech,' 'tale,' 'song,' 'line of verse,' or 'epic poetry as a whole.' All are breathable, the edges are irrelevant.[4]

So Dawes was a man of frames in this way too. He brought edged words to the Sydney people. He was a man of the page, where the printed word gets typeset and held fast. Although he was not typical, he was typological.

Yes and no. As noted in a previous chapter, Dawes was an innovator. His unorthodoxy, presumably, was what set him apart in the regard of the local Aborigines and led him to being accepted and taught by a significant number of them. Furthermore, he was a marine, a man trained to know slipperiness and indeterminacy, trained to have no reliance on solidity, to move back and forth between contradictory determining conditions.

So now we can understand how he sustained his existence amidst so many frames, tagged by so many roles or types: he was not set by them; rather he shuttled within them – mercurial, unsettled.

Moreover with his work on the page, he was always reneging and redrafting. He used the pencil (with all the transience it afforded) as much as he used the permanence of the inked pen. Frequently in the notebooks, he sketched and erased, underscored and overscored in penciled 'rough hand'. He set down the edged words, but he worried and blurred them too.

To say this another way, he was loath to endorse the nominalist account of worldly experience, the account that Dr Johnson – the great list-maker – had affirmed so famously (in James Boswell's account) when he refuted Bishop Berekley's relativistic thinking by kicking a roadside stone and declaring it the basis of the Johnsonian worldview. With a pragmatic, Newtonian and therefore utterly British construal of existence, nouns put labels on objects. In this version of reality, objects wait for sovereign speakers to exert influence on them, to exploit them with verbs and to deploy adjectives in superficial adjustment of their qualities.

Dawes found that such a 'solid state' reality did not hold when he was with the Sydney people. The most telling moment in his language notebooks comes when he noticed there were different ways of speaking in the first-person-plural, depending on whether the speaker was referring to 'we two' or to 'we all'. Moreover, the laws were vehemently strict, demanding that the speaker invoke the collectivity in exactly the right way. To emphasise this point, at one stage the indigene known as Patyegarang – Dawes' principle instructor on the workings of the language – took pains to instruct him to adjust the record of her speech, when she realised that she had not noticed that someone extra (a young girl named Pundul) had been in the scene when they had been talking earlier. This is perhaps the major epiphany Dawes experienced with the Sydney people.[5]

Noting Patyegarang's attentiveness to collectivity reminds me of a remarkable lecture that I witnessed in 1995 at the Museum of Sydney, where the Aboriginal Elder Gerry Bostock interpreted several First Fleet paintings by concentrating on the relative spatial and postural arrangements of groups of Indigenous figures portrayed in the scenes. Understanding how subjectivity can operate in such a collective and integrative manner, one senses mutual responsibility coursing forcefully amongst all objects and subjects in space and time, so much so that the entities an Englishman might want to call 'objects' (animal, mineral and vegetable) are indeed always potentially 'subjects' and 'agents' too. Bostock spent careful time explaining how (probably unbeknown to the painter) at least one of the group-scenes showed a medicinal ceremony in which Indigenes were attending to exactly this restoration of balance in the worldly forces that move through bodies, trees, landmarks and all the other elements that make up a tract of country. Configured this way, the world is always ready to alter, to recalibrate, depending on how the elements are assembled, relative to one another, in any specific place at any particular moment. So it is, too, with the language that represents and transacts this world to all participants: the language must have changefulness in its grammar, it must be relationally motile in its every operation. For the language actively shapes the world even as the words also passively represent whatever is happening.

The linguist Robert Dixon has noted that this recursive quickness is characteristic of most Aboriginal languages in Australia. Because words breathe the awesome power that always rushes all directions through the world, native speakers tend to use generic terms so that their specific meanings within a particular statement have to be apprehended according to the protective context of knowledge shared and agreed by the speaker and the addressees. Thus a word that, on first hearing, might seem to mean 'knee' can also mean many other instances of conjunction, suppleness, folding or turning, depending on the surrounding verbal system in which it is being deployed.[6] With the Indigenous languages, every assertion tends to be specifically contextual, exactly environmental. Every moment of utterance is always colluding with the world as a forceful event rather than accounting for the world as a composite set of given objects or resources merely represented. Aboriginal words tend away from being nominalist, therefore; they tend not to imply a rigid concordance to some locked-off or given world. Instead words are treated in a more 'gaseous' manner, especially in the way they take their shape and weight from everything else around them. This is because the world transmogrifies like that too, having at least as much spirit in it as matter. The world is not only something with status; it has dynamics. It alters from moment to moment, from utterance to utterance, from relational configuration to configuration.

In his bravura essay 'Nominalist and Realist' – written for a markedly different context – Ralph Waldo Emerson said it with riddles, but in a way that is germane to the mutability that Dixon has described and that Dawes experienced:

> Really, all things and persons are related to us, but according to our nature they act on us not at once but in succession, and we are made aware of their presence one at a time. All persons, all things which we have known, are here present, and many more than we see; the world is full … No sentence will hold the whole truth, and the only way in which we can be just, is by giving ourselves the lie; Speech is better than silence; silence is better than speech;—All things are in contact; every atom has a sphere of repulsion;—Things are, and are not, at the same time.[7]

All things are in contact! Generally speaking, in Aboriginal languages there is a heightened awareness of the potential for fundamental realignment in any set of elements, in any prevailing condition. Typically, just as wood might burn to make fire and an animal is ready to become meat, so a single 'lexeme' can refer to wood as well as fire, or to animal as well as meat. With this dramatisation of potentiality, every speakable thing and every action must be understood not as something pre-formed that gets merely qualified or modified by minor adjustments from the outside. Rather, every portion of the world is inextricable from every other portion and must be construed as part of a set of changeful possibilities, all interdependent and constantly determined by environmental conditions.[8] Transmogrification is the rule. Wood can be fire. Rain can be blood. An animal can decease and seem waste but in its death it can become a new push of life when it changes to meat for a man or some other kind of beast.

In the particular case of the Dawes notebooks, Indigenous Sydney nouns and verbs certainly appear less self-contained and solid than English words. The linguist Jeremy Steele, in his exhaustive analysis of the vestiges of the Sydney languages, notes that factors called 'stem-forming suffixes' probably organized most local verbs, which transformed and integrated everything around them, depending on the natural, social and linguistic influences that were prevailing in any scenario from moment to moment.[9] The notebooks suggest that all entities in existence undulate somehow through an endless, multi-directional negotiation with some shifting system of valency that courses amongst all the elements that comprise the lively world. (For example, Patyegarang was known as a grey kangaroo when she was not being named by the three other appellations that Dawes recorded for her; another example, the influential broker, Bennelong, was several different entities at different times and places, with different people.) This is why Dawes took note not only of a solid world made up of named things (hence the nouns in the word-list section of his notebooks), but he also noted how these things changed their qualities and sometimes changed their very names and activeness depending on their relationship to everything else in the lively world. Hence his need to catch the event grammar in narrative vignettes, once he understood some of the different ways to treat the verbs and the scenarios that he had gathered.

Dawes glimpsed a world always transmogrifying, always seeking quick, contingent form as people and things amalgamated and separated within the larger, coursing influence and confluence of the ever-integrating and constantly adjusting grammar of existence. Here was a world where almost nothing could be settled and typified for long stretches of time. Here was a world served by cultural, linguistic and aesthetic forms attuned to mutability. A world understood via changescapes.

These relational operations make models of matter and moments in ways that are radically different from the additive procedures that are applied to sovereign and pre-defined objects, as tends to happen in more 'solid-state' systems such as the English language. The charge-surging, shape-shifting logic that Dawes noticed in the Sydney language (and in cultural configurations such as song-performances and assemblage protocols) is radically at odds with nominalist stabilities. Relational valencies like these – almost electro-magnetic and cybernetic in their logic – were discussed in 1834 by L. E. Threlkeld after he had spent years sampling and analysing the languages of the tribes on the coast north of Sydney. In his cryptic pronouncements, Threlkeld mentioned a 'power' that the language tries to obey and convey:

> the supposition [is] that every sound forms a root, and, consequently, that every character which represents those sounds becomes, likewise, a visible root, so that every letter of the Alphabet of the language is in reality a root, conveying an abstract idea of certain prominent powers which are essential to it.[10]

Threlkeld's belief – that this abstract and flowing 'power' defines coastal languages of the people who worked the tidal pulses and shifting breezes – has been treated by most linguists as fanciful, not to say foolish and heretical, during most of the past century. Even so, his ideas resonate with the Dawes notebooks.

They resonate too with another imaginative rumination on Aboriginal languages and philosophies, namely Barry Hill's great book *Broken Song*, which assays the many enigmas in the life and work of the anthropologist T. G. H. Strehlow. Granted, Sydney Cove is a world away from the Central Australian culture that Strehlow studied, and care must be taken with quick comparisons, but when Hill portrays the challenges for a European mind trying to grasp the somewhat meteorological flows of consciousness out west in the deserts, one cannot help but imagine Dawes on the observatory bluff:

> In general, what Strehlow was contending with … [was the] cryptic and various forms of living knowledge. Gesture, song, whispers, drawing, silence, shifts of sound and sense, the named and unnameable, tacit presuppositions, signs that only stand in the right place, signs that lived in music not in nests of other words alone – all this not to mention dance and elaborate ritual … the embodied nature of Aboriginal signs.[11]

'Signs that lived in music, not in nests of other words alone.' At the start of Dawes' second language notebook, mirroring how the first notebook had commenced with examinations of the verb 'to see', Dawes sets down several notes about *hearing*. Scratched all over the page are detailed rules for the pronunciation of Sydney language, rules distilled from intense listening. This first page is an indication of how much he was valuing immateriality by now, how attentive he had become to ephemeral moments pulsing and drifting away in air. Whereas the first language notebook started with Dawes *looking out over space,* learning from the locals what it means to see, the second notebook starts with Dawes *listening in time,* leaning towards his collaborators, harking to syllables that surge in a moment then waft back to silence; we notice him straining to hear, again and again in the second notebook, as new notes are uttered and then fall away with the next moment while he seeks some pattern in large washes of pronunciation slipping through the vivid, mercurial air that is always basting the harbour.

Then you notice something else extraordinary on the first page of the second notebook. At the top of the sheet, so faint as to be ghostly, as if he is reticent to offer it, Dawes has transcribed in thin pencil the record of a song. In just three word-strings, the intricate phrasing makes sinuous mellifluence. You can imagine the song repeating and rolling for minutes at a time, folding back around on itself in recitation to create an extended, breathy chant. You can imagine a thrilling version delivered as a kind of call and response involving solo and choral interchanges. Or there might have been polyphonic renditions, with full groups of chanters playing with phrase patterns spread across echoic, performative space.

Lingering over this song atop the page you have to use your imagination, because Dawes provides no context for the singing. It is as if he is concealing it even as he reveals it. The reticent pencil markings almost disappear in relation to strong ink strokes that declare the explicit rules of pronunciation all over the rest of the page. Is he making sure the song looks like a secret, like something that cannot be contained, cannot be framed? Is it something not to be made public? Even to himself? The song has no presence, but you know it is there. Nor is any provenance offered for it. Metaphorically speaking, no label sticks to it. And no translation is supplied. It is properly vaporous and inscrutable but undeniably important.

In fact, three times in the second notebook, as he becomes increasingly enmeshed in the intimate narratives of Indigenous days and nights, songs swirl around Dawes. However, avid as he usually is to offer his account of every event, he never gets or gives meanings for the songs. Dawes offers no gloss on the settings, no notes about the performances, no quick interpretations. This is telling. Most likely, Dawes was beginning to understand that he could not be so presumptuous as to ask just any pointed question about a force as elemental and activating as a song.

How to register the powerful strangeness and sacredness of vocal music moving the air about? In the brief duration of its conjuring, a song makes a world by setting sound and tempo in cooperation against the larger, messier sloshes of time, danger, mortality and the forces of generational increase. How to understand the breathy, spiritual powers – the respiration and the inspiration – that were set in motion when people used their voices like this to make and hear music? How to catch such oral coruscation, to sense not only what a song divulges but more importantly, perhaps, what it might also be designed to conceal? Can you sense this, first, and then can you convey it with proper force, using any mode of communication other than the song itself?

Throughout *Broken Song,* Barry Hill explains how chants, recitations and songs in Central Australia often exerted a kind of 'masking' work on the domain where they were performed. In the Arrente culture that Hill studies, the connections that make knowledge are stored and distributed as memory-prompts encompassing many people throughout vast tracts of country across seasonal rotations of time. Moreover, the knowledge that the Arrente generate and hold communally is powerful and fearsome. This knowledge is connected to forces that hold the world together and also threaten to destroy it. In proximity to such power, individual singers and listeners need to keep large portions of knowledge unconscious, or secret, or sequestered from the uninitiated. To be flippant with such forceful knowledge is to risk the spirit not just of your singularly embodied self but of the entire, sentient world that wraps around and infuses every spirit-charged component of any scene. Which means the songs must function as sophisticated 'technologies' for holding and releasing information-as-cosmic-force without giving it to just anyone and everyone. Damage could too easily occur – to the information, to the people receiving it and to the world that transmits the huge forces organizing existence. Truly this is an awesome world; and truly to sing is to undertake something awe-full.

After all, information is the most important thing people in oral culture have: information about how to live. Taking care of this information, keeping it always ready, is the main task of culture. The knowledge synthesized from all the kept information is so vast, distributed and all-insinuating that no one person can know everything. When the full system of knowledge is well managed, individuals might carry and keep specific portions of information that can curl and cinch together in communal ceremonies and testimonies so that the full community will always know far more than any single person can receive and comprehend. Secrecy makes intrigue and it generates a memorable 'charge' of danger for everyone worrying over how to preserve and respect the information. Secrecy ensures that knowledge is desirable but also that it is dreadful and revered. And in a practical routine that boosts memorial efficiency across an entire society that so vitally needs a full store of knowledge in order to survive in a demanding environment, the rules of secrecy can govern how different portions of the society conjoin in ceremony at different times. In Arrente song-sessions, for example, information is maintained, refreshed, exchanged and joined up to guarantee the effective distribution of larger systems of knowledge across the entire configuration of the community. Accessing all the dismembered portions of information that various individuals carry into ceremony, the full community remembers forcefully. Songs are vital to this communal remembrance. And they work by leaving some things unsaid at particular moments.

In the traditional Arrente systems that Hill studies, the force of the cosmos gets channeled and worshipped in language: 'the secret-sacred word was masked in two ways: acoustically and semantically.' There is a special power in the acoustics of a song because a secret-sacred word 'could be disguised by the rhythm and measure of the song' in such a way that the semantics could be present but covert, 'subject to syllabic disguise' created by tempo, rhythm and rhyme. This means there can be enormous power in a syllable, a spoken one or an unspoken one. With each new performance, 'syllables might be added, vowels might be broken, speech accents eliminated' and the known world would thus get re-configured and re-proposed by something so slight yet enormous as the injection or extraction of a vocable suffix, just for that one context, just for that one performed instant.[12]

There is no way of knowing for sure if it was like this with the singing that was performed by the Sydney people. But there is clear evidence that the people were extremely attentive to the conditions in which vocalisation occurs, especially loudly projected utterance. For example, there is the strange incident – strange to Dawes, at least – in the second notebook, when the lieutenant sings a song to his native companions and their response is not delight or gratitude or curiosity, but anger. Evidently, songs were not to be offered or received lightly. They were meant to happen only when propitious. Songs were directly connected to cosmic force, given how they were emphatic and expansive utterance, given how they caused the dramatic arousal of the air. Dawes did not know this at first.

Most important of all is the instance when Patyegarang corrected the record of what she had said sometime earlier when she had not taken full account of all the people who had been listening. Dawes noted here a complexity in the multiple ways the Sydney people were able to say 'we', testifying to how attentive they were to the composition of the audience in any place and any time they fashioned a public statement. This caution would have been acute when a song was involved. Most likely the Sydney people operated in much the same way that Hill describes in relation to the Arrente customs. Most likely they simply declined to translate their songs for Dawes, or to give him any context, because the people kept at least a few secrets in and around some of their songs and because they were protecting him – uninitiated as he was – from the force of them.

By listening to the singing, the rightly initiated people could maintain strong their world-sustaining memory; they could get quick, emphatic reminders of what they had to think about, what they had to recall, what they had to communicate, what they had to obey, to revere and to fear not only in the moment of hearing but through all time. (Notably, in the second notebook [p. 15], Dawes records the word 'ngara' and explains that it means not only to hear or listen, but also to think.) Dawes must have noticed how little information the people were prepared to divulge to him about these dramatic, highly expressive interludes. Certainly the reader notices, by default, how exceptional these sung scenes are; the reader notices how, elsewhere in the notebooks, Dawes is keen to offer contextual details and clipped narratives associated with spoken and sometimes whispered utterances that he has been offered. But with the songs that buffeted loud around him, as intriguing and ardent as they seem, we get nothing.

On the second page of the second notebook, directly facing where Dawes records the three-word song and gives no translation of it but gives thorough details about rules of pronunciation, he also sketches a faint map and offers terms for 'the four winds'. Song, country, laws, and the many ways the world's ceaseless breath can get ranged across and rearranged all about existence! Such enormities flitted across these pages! Remembering that spirit is just another word for breath (this is the case even in a language so 'statusfied' and materially predisposed as English), we can see how Dawes inaugurates the second notebook with great spiritual force, with the pushing animus of life, with eros, with something burgeoning, something uncontainable.

This leads us to another telling interlude in the second notebook (pp. 11 and 12) when Dawes considers the transformational work afforded by the sound 'kara'. Scattered throughout the various records of the coastal languages that were recorded during the colonial years (not only by Dawes but also by several other language-catchers several decades after he had gone), we find these words that have been empowered by these two syllables:

Karaga – to pronounce, to utter, to urge meaningful breath out from oneself and into the world

Karadigan – a doctor, a healer, one who works with the fertile and beneficial forces burgeoning in the world

Karamung – a swelling, an upwelling, as in water or in a wound

Karangan – fingernails, growing out from the body, reaching into the larger world

Karabul – the cutting edge or back of a sword or a tool that pushes into the world's matter and changes beneficially

Karal – a snood or a covering that receives and protects the incisive, penetrating end of a hook

Karabi – the screeching cockatoo bird, the one whose flight and amplifying call can take over the sky

Karama – to profit by stealing

Karau – testicles.

(The references for 'stealing' and 'testicles' are derived from R H Mathews' later word list, circa 1901. Acknowledgements to the database in Jeremy Steele's *The Aboriginal Language of Sydney*.)

Dawes recorded many words like these, words and phrases that witnessed a force for growth and benefaction in the country. There is a sense in 'kara' of something that is characteristic of the Sydney region: the thrilling sense of increase or burgeon. When the suffix 'kara' insinuates a phrase, the world the phrase represents seems to reconfigure and rouse through the language. Any utterance that gets reorganised by 'kara' seems to carry the world's force. The uttered world benefits from a linguistic energy that shadows the physical and metaphysical energy of the country. The 'kara' force seemed to work into everything, including the language itself, which was the means whereby the Sydney people literally pronounced and pushed the vitality all around them. The 'kara' force moved through every aspect of their world – though people, tools, plants, animals, actions, ideas and emotions – all of which were described with 'kara'-infused words. This 'kara' force was a suffusing influence, a potentiality always moving and changing. It was the pushing insistence of fertility. It was an urge bringing vitality, opposing the stillness, contractions and desiccations of fear and death. If you know the Sydney ecology, if you know, for instance, that dizzying burst of fertility that flares when certain acacia 'come on' suddenly overnight and the birds and insects throng and thrum around the fresh aromatic nectar, then you have a sense of how 'kara' can steep one's comprehension.

The way Dawes treated the songs that he recorded suggests he registered some of this 'kara' force. He seemed to sense it in the language too, especially in the way many suffixes – not only 'kara' – could push backwards and forwards in utterance and bring change to all the words transpiring in the air, as if the words themselves formed an amenable human climate that served the cosmic-scaled environment.

Dawes came to appreciate the rush of increase, the burgeon and boundlessness of the Sydney environment. Ready as he was to loosen his frames, ready because of his paradoxical make-up and because of the contradictions that he felt when he associated both with the invaders and with the Indigenes, Dawes knew himself eventually as someone cast against type, someone more dynamic than static, uncontained by received, rigid frames.

The local language pushed him that way, out of tight bounds. It was the extensity as much as the intensity of his feelings when he spoke with the Sydney people that caused him, finally, to abjure his colonial mission. He was altered by the intimacy and the peculiar local hedonism that the Sydney people offered him. All this vividness broke his frames and shifted his status: the sensory lushness of twilights at harbor-cove beaches; the feasts of charcoal-roasted shellfish and seafood; the languid moonlighted evenings bushwalking on the headlands; the nights scintillated by a billion stars shivering the far sky; the air enriched surprisingly by special songs amplifying under the near sky; the moving intimacy of his transactions with Patyegarang.

All these sensory charges put change in him and cast him away from the typeset roles he seemed initially to have been fitted for. All these sensations led him to the most notorious thing he did in Sydney: the repeated and public insubordination that he threw at Governor Arthur Phillip, when Phillip ordered Dawes to become the military man again, the conquistador, when Phillip ordered him to go out hunting local tribes, and Dawes refused, knowing that he would be traduced in the colony and in England, knowing that he had willfully destroyed all the colonial frames that he had once yearned to have around him. Something he experienced with the Indigenes threw him out of the most profitable of his pre-ordained types and over into one last frame: finally he was cast by his colonial directors as the recalcitrant, the pariah. Governor Phillip pushed him out of the colony. All the great prizes that Dawes had once presumed to be within reach, they all went elsewhere from him now. The self he once thought was waiting, pre-defined for him: this self was somebody other than him by the time he had felt and been shifted by the full erotics of the Sydney experience

Anne Carson helps us understand the full impact of this hedonism. Reminding us of the sense-constraining rigours that were expected of the focused man of the page, Carson's ideas can help us imagine how fixity must have cracked around and within Dawes amidst the thrilling intimacies that he was accorded by the locals at Sydney Cove:

> Literate training encourages a heightened awareness of physical boundaries and a sense of those boundaries as the vessel of one's self. To control the boundaries is to possess oneself. For individuals to whom self-possession has become important, the influx of a sudden, strong emotion from without cannot be an unalarming event ... When an individual appreciates that he alone is responsible for the content and coherence of his person, an influx of eros becomes a concrete personal threat.[13]

Given all the poignancy and piquancy that intensified his Sydney days and nights, Dawes would have felt this erotic challenge to his coherence upwelling as some kind of kara-force. It would have felt like the end of one English world in and around him. Catastrophic and cauterizing as it would have felt to the straitlaced methodiser within him, it clearly also felt like the chance to go otherwise, to go into changefulness, to flow into a restless process of self-realisation and environmental increase. The one frame that fitted him, finally, was porous at its edges: with the Eora he grew to operate in a changescape.

### Notes

1    Anne Carson, *EROS the bittersweet: an essay*. Princeton, NJ: Princeton University Press, 1986, p. 43.

2   Carson, p. 44.
3   Carson, p. 44.
4   Carson, p. 50.
5   William Dawes, The Language Notebooks 1 and 2, created in 1791, accessible at http://www.dnathan.com/eprints/dnathan_etal_2009_dawes.pdf, Notebook 2, p. 35.
6   Robert Dixon, *Australian Languages: their nature and development*, Cambridge: Cambridge University Press, 2002, p. 59.
7   Ralph Waldo Emerson, 'Nominalist and Realist', (first published 1844), anthologized in *The Complete Prose Works*, London: Ward, Lock and Co, 1891, p.150.
8   Dixon, pp. 59–62.
9   Jeremy Steele, *The Aboriginal Language of Sydney: a partial reconstruction of the indigenous language of Sydney based on the notebooks of William Dawes of 1790–91, informed by other records of the Sydney and surrounding languages to c. 1905*. Sydney: Macquarie University MA Thesis, 2005, pp. 211–21.
10  L.E. Threlkeld, *An Australian language as spoken by the Awabakal, the people of Awaba or Lake Macquarie (near Newcastle, New South Wales) being an account of their language, traditions and customs*, edited and abridged by John Fraser, Sydney: NSW Government Printer, 1892, p. 90.
11  Barry Hill, *Broken Song: T.G.H. Strehlow and Aboriginal Possession*, Sydney: Random House, 2002, p. 176.
12  Hill, p. 435.
13  Carson, pp. 44–5.

## 12

## WHAT THE EYE CAN HEAR

There is a vivid moment in Barry Hill's *Broken Song* when he quotes a few translated verses from a chant that, under particular social and spiritual conditions, used to be intoned across Arrente country in the MacDonnell Ranges of Central Australia. It is a brief sequence depicting eagles, lasting just a few moments but suggesting enormities:

> One above the other we are hovering in the air
> Both of us are hovering in the air
> Off the edge of the mountain bluff we are hovering
>   in the air
> Near the jagged mountain edge we are hovering
>   in the air.[1]

Note all the different senses zinging in these verses: the keen and extensive vision, the sonic buffeting of winds and wings, the smell of the desert ozone, the rhythmic connotations of flapping and gliding, the haptics in the serrations depicted below and the gusts and the heat ready all around to sear away skin. There is also the special sense that sportspeople sometimes mention—proprioception—whereby you understand your relative position within a dynamic field by registering your own body's ever-altering alignments in interplay with everything else that is shifting around you and 'addressing' you in space and time.

Looking at these four lines of song on the page, you can imagine the rhythms making a performance. In your mind's ear you can hear how the singers might decline to utter particular words or phrases during a few instants while the song carries on until language can be offered again to public audition, or how the clapping might stall for a moment but then recommence by picking up the lapsed but implicit beat when the time was right. You can imagine how one sense might 'cover' but also represent another for a while, until the context is made right for bringing the temporarily 'concealed' element back into explicit play. As Hill explains, secrets could be 'masked in two ways: acoustically and semantically'. There is a special power in the acoustics of the declamations because a sacred word 'could be disguised by the rhythm and measure of the song' in such a manner that the semantics could be present but covert, 'subject to syllabic disguise' created by tempo, rhythm and rhyme. This means there can be enormous power in a sound, whether uttered or kept quiet. With each new performance, 'syllables might be added, vowels might be broken, speech accents eliminated' and the known world could thus get re-configured and re-proposed, just for that one participant context, that one performed instant in the endless flux of the world's experience in time.[2]

In their systematic entirety, the song cycles would have conveyed secret and sacred elements. And nowadays outsiders should always be worried when taking exemplary bits of the great epics into a new context. But this is partly what Hill investigates throughout his mighty book: how the songs are stronger and smarter than any novice can know, and how if they are witnessed respectfully, in a repeated and applied way, the songs can bring knowledge slowly into the untutored mind.

Moreover, and this is the genius of them, the songs hold secrets that do not get divulged to people unprepared for their import. Even as they seem to be explicitly unfolding, vital portions of the chants can arc right past the people who should not receive them. The songs can say without uttering, they can show without revealing. They can do this by mingling different senses so that something heard or unheard might refer to something seen or unseen; or something felt in choreographic motion within the participant's nervous system might be the key to remembering a phrase that needs to be uttered but must be kept silent if the wrong people are around. Significant tenets can be remembered and testified by coding and trading them (or by trammelling them) *across* the senses. Thus a secret sound can be kept quiet but alive in a gesture; or a sacred painted pattern can be represented in a chanted rhythm in such a way that the crucial information is conveyed only to people who already know it, who have earned rights to be with it, who have already been brought inside the secret of it. Ignorant people will miss the meaning of the gesture, or fail to hear the thing that should be seen or felt, and no harm will get done to them or to the larger system of knowledge that is being forever maintained through all these varied mnemonic practices.

With such rich, strategic synaesthesia – because of how a song cycle is made of so many 'multi-modal' interrelations – the senses become altogether inseparable, infinitely layered and communicative. Significance arises relationally, within a network of activated and intersected senses. Please note: I am referring to synaesthesia not as a syndrome, not as some affliction or blessing visited upon an exceptional outsider. Rather, in this context synaesthesia is a culturally endorsed and trained capability. It is a technical ability deployed for communicative and mnemonic purposes. Which means that a singular, separated notion such as 'visuality' is important in the maintenance and conveyance of meaning, but it is not pre-eminent and it cannot be discussed in isolation from the meshed panoply of all the other senses.

This notion of synaesthesiac virtuosity chimed for me a while ago when I was listening to Martin Thomas's superb radio compositions responding to the life and work of Jimmie Barker, the great Aboriginal archivist and sound artist of Muruwari heritage (from Western New South Wales, around Brewarrina).[3] Late in his life Barker taught himself the art of audio recording and commenced an extraordinary project of language-gathering and storytelling which eventually accrued into an archive of more than two hundred hours, comprised mostly of Barker's mellifluous solo voice 'playing' the microphone in simple but utterly compelling ways. In a quiet room at home, Barker would speak into his recorder, slowly and with immense authority, humility, and musicality. This was mostly in 1970. Almost half a century later, the listener senses his presence, or more exactly the listener senses both his *persistence* and the continuity of his remembered culture. In Barker's voice—in the music of it and in the somatic delicacy of the utterance of it—a listener gets a palpable sense, something registering in the body as well as in the semantic sections of one's intellect. For example, there is a subtle synaesthetic trope performed in a brief moment on one of the language-tapes where Barker records the word for a comet: '*Bunda_gaan*—meaning: comet ... sky snake ... *Bunda_gaan* ... sky snake meaning a comet ... known also as *duun_birra mirrin* ... *duun_birra mirrin*: star with a tail.' The crucial aspect of the recording is the way Barker breathes and sustains the words, then repeats them with new tempo and an adjusted tone, and then offers another way—a spoken way, a breathed, *embodied* way—simultaneously to see, hear and feel the comet's form and motion across the sky. He says 'Bunda_gaan' and says it again slightly differently, so that you the listener can see it up there and can see it again anew and changed—this sky snake—in a slightly different part of the sky now! He says 'duun_birra mirrin' and then says 'staaarr ... with a taaiiillll' so that you can sense the shape, the stretch and the slow momentum of the comet in your mind's eye even as you cannot really see it. There is an extending, bodily gesture is the phrasing. In other words, you get to jump senses and grasp the phenomenon of the comet via your faculty of sound and within your pulsing nervous system, where rhythm resides, so that you can understand the trailing, time-soaked exhaust of it in cosmic motion up there!

At the start of *Broken Song*, Barry Hill proclaims a kind of manifesto concerning not only his own work as a poet but also the work of Aboriginal singing that he seeks to analyse. Language, he reminds us, 'is a somatic act before it is anything else.' From the first instance we encounter it, 'language goes into the ear before anything else and all our attempts to understand its speakers are bound up with bodies in space together, with a form approaching intimacy. Bodies sing in the company of voices.'[4] So, language is not only a heard thing. It is also muscular and neurological. And it is temporal and spatial. It is choreographic therefore. Synaesthetic, therefore. Visual, auditory, proprioceptive, inextricably poly-sensory, therefore.

To pause and take stock for a moment, let me observe how I have been taking examples from across a broad spectrum of Aboriginal cultures—from Arrente to Muruwari—how I have been knocking notions together in a montage fashion that is thought-provoking and questionable. Literally, technically questionable. Not being a linguist, nor an anthropologist, nor Aboriginal, this 'troubling' (to use a splendid Aboriginal-English word) is all I can claim to do: raise some useful questions and offer some debatable answers, some propositions to think with. I have no conclusive thesis, nothing to stop debate or put an end to the arguments. Standing at the outside edge of these issues concerning Aboriginal culture, I have no authority to proclaim any incontrovertible meanings from within that culture. But I do have some rights to wonder about what happened and continues to happen when two mostly opposite worlds—the Indigenous and the Incursive—come into contact. Mostly, what happens is that questions arise, some values get erased and mysteries abound. And sometimes, interrogations and accountable speculations serve to generate something useful from the befuddlement. So this is the sum of my currency: questions, not conclusive decrees, about moments of contact, translation, eradication and reverberation.

Questions about how the several senses mesh to make meaning have been proliferating for me during the twenty years or more that I have been pondering another virtuosic language archive: the notebooks that developed out of the research conducted into the Indigenous language of Sydney Cove, by the engineer, astronomer and marine lieutenant William Dawes, during the years 1788 till 1791.

As I indicated in the previous chapter, Dawes set himself apart during most of his four years as an officer of the First Fleet at Sydney Cove. In character and activity, he set himself apart from the convicts and the rest of the troops and officers. Paradoxically, as he did so, he became enmeshed with a select community of approximately twenty Indigenous people of all ages, who sought him out and clearly preferred him to all the other newcomers. Installed at the tiny astronomer's observatory that Governor

Arthur Phillip had commissioned soon after the marines had seized the only steady stream and all the lofty vantage points around the Cove, Dawes worked late into most nights. He spent candle-lit hours star-gazing and calculating, sometimes accompanied by native acquaintances. Where the southern stanchions of the Sydney Harbour Bridge now stamp the earth, that is where he lived, just out of shouting distance from the site of Governor Phillip's headquarters near present-day Circular Quay, a thousand paces around an arc of shoreline.

At Sydney Cove, the Indigenous people offered Dawes courtesies and some batches of knowledge, such that he started to understand a local mentality that was organized both around a directly felt sense of connectedness to place and through a distributed or networked sense of relatedness amongst all the people and sentient beings and energised objects in that place. He began to sense how all beings might connect, communicate and be interdependently cognate. This sense of profuse meaning and identity flowing in a capillary fashion all across a place encouraged in him an immersive relationship to the world. He caught enough evidence to indicate that this sense of relationship was sustained in Eora country both as an intelligence shared with all matter and as an attentiveness to the collective integrity and vitality of the full complement of people who comprise the society that wraps around and carries all participants through this lively world. This was a mode of existence quite at odds with his logical, engineer's training. It was a shift in consciousness that seems to have worked into him with a revelatory force which changed his values and his codes of action.

As he encountered the people of Sydney Cove (the Eora), Dawes compiled two language notebooks, one dedicated mostly to lists of clipped nouns and verbs, the other dedicated to a more complex investigation of social relationships and scenarios that Dawes often explained *narratively* rather than analytically. Dawes started the first notebook with several pages covering the declensions of the verb 'naa: to see'. Clearly, visual perception and cognition were a major concern for him, surveyor and astronomer as he was. And clearly the Eora knew how to describe and analyse vision: they had much detail to offer Dawes when he asked them what it means for them, to see. But my crucial point is that the sense of sight is not conceivable as something separable from or more highly valued than all the other senses meshed together. This point is emphasised throughout the second notebook, where Dawes pays much attention to hearing, touch and proprioception, where he begins to understand that knowledge often has to be inferred from implication, immersion, distraction and silence, that in relational systems of meaning and value one thing cannot be separated from another, and important portions of existence are not available for distanced, analytical exposure in the way that most European scientists expected.

In the previous chapter, I noted how Dawes seemed, simultaneously, to show and to conceal the importance of Eora songs. Using the faintest whisps of pencil in his notebooks and then overwriting most of these marks with unrelated, inked information about other themes, Dawes puts meagre clues on a few of his pages, first to note how he heard the song and next to make the point that he declines to offer any translation or evaluation. Lingering over the songs in the notebooks, you have to use your imagination, because Dawes provides no precise context for the singing. It is as if he is concealing it even as he reveals it.

Most likely, Dawes was beginning to understand that he had to earn rather than simply record and acquire special caches of knowledge, that he had to grow into it through ritual actions and ordeals performed over many years. How to catch quickly the world-making complexity of music, for example?

As I have already mentioned, in other parts of Indigenous Australia a kind of 'masking' work was often performed by and in songs. With the myriad connections that make knowledge, they all get distributed across many people and throughout vast tracts of country. Moreover, the knowledge that the people all generate and hold communally is powerful and fierce and fearsome.

My point is there is plentiful evidence that Indigenous Australian cultures have always distributed, cared for and guarded against the potential haemorrhaging of all this power by deploying *relational*, changeful and systematic thinking. Which is to say that to differentiate and to hierarchise singular notions such as sight, vision, touch, taste, smell and thought is to miss the systematics and the improvisatory quickness of the 'ecological' and 'synaesthetic' kind of mentality that is always informing Indigenous experience. In the meshed complexity of immersed, environmental existence, of course, we can name each individual sense—for example, 'naa: to see'—and we can *look at* such a spotlighted concept in order to start to know its imbrication within all other modes of cognition. But we cannot know anything in isolation from all the other factors that make the great system of existence. Just as Jimmie Barker could use sound and the embodied governance of breath and his muscular relaxation when he was evoking the experience of regarding a comet, just as the Arrente singers used somatic rhythms and proprioception to give insights about the all-seeing eagle, so we can know the world only by entangling the senses. We can study vision and come to understand it better, but only if we loosen our focus on it, only if we blur vision back into the interconnected, relational system of all the senses, only if we make sense by deliberately agitating one sense to change into another, to make full sense from dynamism.

Imagine the eagles hovering up there: all senses ablaze, all senses supporting and cavorting through one another, the world and the birds caught in a delicate and dynamic balance that holds and folds each of them as one because all the senses are correlating and changing, moment to moment.

## Notes

1. Barry Hill, *Broken Song: T.G.H. Strehlow and Aboriginal Possession*, Random House, Sydney, 2002, p. 14.
2. Hill, *Broken Song*, p. 435.
3. Martin Thomas, drawing from the archives of Jimmie Barker, *This is Jimmie Barker*. ABC Radio, 2000; and *I Love You Jimmie*. ABC Radio, 2001. Note: transcriptions from the audiotapes are my own versions of what I am hearing. The phonetic language is of my own devising, rather than being some linguistically ratified language. The 'comet sequence' comes from the first five minutes of *This is Jimmie Barker*.
4. Hill, *Broken Song*, p. 3.

# 13

# A FOREST. A CLEARING.

## Introduction

This chapter is a brief meditation on the way apprehension can get generated simultaneously 'inside and outside' a phenomenon. I offer some insights learned from making and installing an immersive audiovisual artwork called 'Street X-Rays'[1]. The chapter is thus a report delivering a small quantum of knowledge that was pursued and evidenced in a process of practice-led research, using the development of the artwork as a laboratory for investigating the aesthetic dimensions of historical understanding. To get this knowledge across to you – to name the ideas, meanings and affects generated by the work and to shift them from being tacit within me so that they can become explicit and communicable for you – I will need to describe the artwork.

But first, a couple of stories. Stories about forests. Archetypal places of immersion. Stories to get us thinking about inside and outside, about involvement and critical distance.

## Forest Story #1

Pedro Fernandez de Quiros was a Portuguese mariner who rose to prominence in Spain's imperial navy during the 1600s. Like Christopher Columbus before him, Quiros dedicated his voyage to the Franciscan missionary order.[2] This meant that his explorations were governed by the doctrines narrated in Francis of

Assisi's 'Rule of Life', a text urging devotees to range the earth and convert pagan souls to Christ. St Francis (1182–1226) had envisaged a world order governed by his interpretations of the gospels. Four centuries after their initial decree, these doctrines had become globally influential.

In December, 1605, Quiros led a flotilla west from Callao in Peru, into unknown realms of the Pacific. He seemed well prepared: in case mysteries overwhelmed the voyage, Franciscan chaplains were on board and Quiros took regular counsel from their edicts. Thus even as he was generating *new* knowledge, gleaning it everyday from his investigative procedures, he was also relying on *established* knowledge stored in axioms predetermined by the forces he accepted as authoritative. His new, discovered insights wove into his received wisdom; his evolving, *procedural* understanding meshed with his incumbent, *precepted* understanding.

The ships bumped eventually into the island-cluster which is nowadays called Vanuatu. Quiros dubbed the landfall 'La Austrialia del Espiritu Santo', an elegantly efficient name: it honoured the Holy Ghost, whose feast the voyagers were celebrating on this auspicious Pentecost Sunday, and it also emphasised the Austrian heritage of the Spanish sovereign Philip III whilst simultaneously describing the southerly aspect of the country.

Quiros was convinced he had encountered the east coast of the oft-predicted Terra Australis Incognita and he declared the isles to be the site of a New Jerusalem. For thirty-six days his crew busied themselves establishing a village (called Vera Cruz) on the shores of the harbour where the flotilla took shelter. Boats skiffed back and forth, a slice of open land was cleared in the shoreline, soil was tilled, and the indigenes made sure the newcomers knew they were about.

Fatalities among the islanders seem to have been fewer here than had become customary whenever the European carnival of death visited the 'New Worlds'. Perhaps Quiros insisted on humane behaviour. Perhaps he was being prudent after calculating the overwhelming numbers of Melanesian warriors.

Or perhaps he succumbed to a loss of faith in his principles, contributing to a kind of normless inertia causing inaction. For the reports that have survived from the days at La Austrialia tell of a paralysis of executive will. So close to his presumed Utopia, Quiros seemed unable to 'realise' it, unable to get his ideas and desires matched to the material attributes of this portion of the world. As O.H.K. Spate wrote in his great study of Spanish voyaging, on May 25, the feast day of Corpus Christi, Quiros 'walked a league inland, past the already sprouting gardens he had planted, and on his return casually announced that since they stood little chance against native hostility, they would leave next day and visit the islands to windward'.[3]

No sooner had they weighed anchor than fickle winds freshened and everything went awry on the command ship. There was dissension among the crew and Quiros was stricken with something like catatonia while junior officers seized then lost control of navigation, with the result that the command ship failed to tack into shelter, getting buffeted instead by gales out into the open ocean. Eventually Quiros rallied enough to order the crew to veer north and catch the winds that blew the ship east toward Acapulco, back through ocean tracts already known to him.

Meanwhile, the other ships waited at Vera Cruz until, after days of searching for the commander, Luis Vaes de Torres took charge of the remnant flotilla. He sailed a guesswork course west through uncharted seas toward the Spanish colony in the Philippines and thereby completed the famous voyage across the previously unmapped strait that still bears his name.[4] In Manila, Torres was received as the triumphant conquistador who arrived clutching new charts full of fresh knowledge. In Acapulco, Quiros was shunned as a craven bungler who had brought nothing back to port but shame and irresolution.

What happened in the forest, one league in from the shoreline, on that feast Day of Corpus Christi, 1606?

Quiros never offered details. But it is not difficult or controversial to imagine a plausible scene. Leaving the gridded garden, Quiros ventured into the dense forest. He would have lost visual perspective almost immediately. He would have sensed the uselessness of his surveyor's skills. Unable to rely on straightlined vision to know where he'd just come from, where he was placed right now and where he might go next; losing his coordinates, he would have been assailed by smells and sounds coming at him from every direction. And haptically, the ground under his feet would have been disorienting him with every step. Perhaps he fell into panic. Literally, PANIC – the condition of overwhelming 'everywhereness'. Imagine his sense of self disintegrating while stimuli descended and dispersed around and away from him in all directions at once. He would have felt the indiscriminate wildness around him, the excessive, multi-modal information and threat coming from all quarters, no way to organize or overpower the inputs, no way to apprehend quickly and safely a set of reliable principles in this peculiar environment, if indeed the forest had any principles.

Sensing the sudden inadequacies of his own cognitive systems, Quiros would have felt the need to investigate this 'new' world, to learn its qualities and tendencies. He would have felt compelled to become attuned to it, to be immersed and explorative in it, to feel his own constitution deform and then reform by melding with the environment so that he could alter his consciousness by imbibing the consciousness of the forest. And he would have sensed how little security and guidance he was afforded to do so in this urgent and untethered circumstance. With the indigenous warriors all around him, offering him no safety, no guidelines, he would have felt unable to let go of his precepts despite how inadequate these precepts were proving to be in this deep immersion. He would have felt unable to loosen comportment in order to realign himself to the unaccustomed dynamics and patterns that might have prevailed in the forest. Most likely, he sensed only chaos in the steaming environment and he had no way to get clear of the enveloping stimuli, no way to reflect on the forest, to rationalize it and know some of its peculiar principles before getting engrossed again so as to investigate the profusion further. No way to accede to a careful and orienting rhythm of investigative immersion/reflection/immersion/reflection.

Scampering back to the beach, therefore, Quiros signaled to the ship and aborted the mission, convinced this was not a place that would be readily overlaid with prescribed plans; nor would it allow him to survive the alterations and vulnerabilities implicit to discovering and imbibing local principles.

### Forest Story #2

In the middle of the Nineteenth Century, when Henry David Thoreau went to dwell amidst the woods near Concorde (Massachusetts), he scraped a clearing for himself alongside Walden Pond, and he made a scene for consciousness. Not *only* a metaphor (although it IS a metaphor too), Thoreau's clearing is much more than a place; it's also *an unstable process* in time and space, a blur between the phenomenal world and the noumenal self. Thoreau's clearing at Walden is a delicate instant in a momentary place where intuition, reasoning, speculation and understanding all get a chance to work on and into each other.

In his journal, Thoreau jotted this quick thought: 'You cannot see anything until you are clear of it'.[5] He believed this even as he was convinced that nothing was worth seeing and knowing unless it has been sensed during direct, immersed engagement within the profuse dynamics of the world that holds and produces everything perceptible. Hence the value of the clearing within the forest. Or, as Frederick Garber summarises the riddle, 'Thoreau ... knows that a part of the self must have a direct and immediate relationship with experience, or the observer will have nothing at all to see.'[6] The clearing must be *within,* not *instead of* the forest; the clearing must be *part of* and *not set apart from* all the tumult that makes dynamic experience. The clearing is useful because it is never completely clear even as it affords instants of clarity.

So Thoreau was convinced of the need for what he called 'doubleness', the need to be always simultaneously immersed but also reflective whilst trying to know the world and oneself, trying to know the world as oneself, trying to know the self in the world. Which is not quite the same as trying to know the self *as* the world. Quoting Garber again, we can see how the act of knowing is delicate and ephemeral when it is at its most telling, for example when Thoreau is in his clearing, simultaneously immersed and reflective:

> The act [of knowing] is both a discovery about what the world is like (or ought to be) and what he himself is like. In the same act he organises his perception of himself and of his world. A clearing in the forest is not only an instance of what consciousness can do, redeeming a piece of nature; it is also an image of the

redeeming consciousness itself, the cleared space within which one stands and does one's relating to experience. Furthermore, whatever consciousness gains through these creative acts leads to an increase in the content of the mind.[7]

For Thoreau, there must be an interplay between one's own shaped (and shaping) mentality, in one plane of reality, and the dynamic liveliness of the world, in a different but simultaneously active plane of reality. Only by interlacing these cognitively separate modes of experience – the mode of one's own self and the mode of the world's plenitude – only by combining them whilst paradoxically also discerning their distinctions, only then can we get to some valid notion of how the world is arranged for us, in us, by us and despite us, in all the world's complexity and mutability. As Thoreau wrote in his account of *A Week on the Concord and Merrimack Rivers*:

> Observation is so wide awake, and facts are being so rapidly added to the sum of human experience, that it appears as if the theorizer would always be in arrears, and were doomed forever to arrive at imperfect conclusions; but the power to perceive a law is equally rare in all ages of the world, and depends but little on the number of facts observed.

In other words, Thoreau understands the need to look for patterns within the flux of experience. By discerning such patterns, one might comprehend some principles that momentarily organise the world, even at the same time as one knows that change is always assailing every shape in the world, to the extent that patterns and principles must be understood to be temporary and contingent on more factors than any one human mentality will ever encompass.

(Note: if you want a third forest story that offers some views, different again, into these same themes, you could flick back to Chapter One, to the account of John Grosser's beautiful sawmill in the Pilliga Scrub.)

### The Moral of the Stories

Which brings us to the moral of the forest stories, as we close in on our contemplation of the dynamic-immersive artwork called 'Street X-Rays'.

For Quiros and Thoreau – the former in flight from new realizations, the latter wanting to see deeply into beckoning complexities – each sensed that he needed to be both inside and outside the experiences and objects that he was trying to understand. Each sensed the need for both a *procedural* (or heuristic) path to fresh knowledge and a *principled* (or didactic) reliance on what is already known. Each sensed that the more avidly he engaged in procedural knowing, the more elastic many of his given principles must become. And each sensed that to go into a scene with no principles prescribed would be to invite madness, incomprehension, panic.

Quiros felt the danger extremely and he recoiled from the prospect. Thoreau, on the other hand, figured how to conserve and alter himself as he absorbed the challenges of his immersive environment.

Herein lies another moral, one that takes us to questions of art. Immersive, dynamic art-environments are phenomena designed like eco-systems, to put us in complexity but to put us there with sufficient care and personal security so that we stand a chance of comprehending some of the tendencies in the system.

In other words, when we sense an instability or mutability in such an artwork, within these safe havens we can concentrate on the qualities of that instability rather than on personal dangers associated with unpredictability. The artwork is thus an investigative, contemplative, environment, closer to Thoreau's sojourn than Quiros' panic in the forest.

As noted in an earlier chapter, the artist David Rokeby has observed that immersive, interactive installations are best understood not as *finished artworks* but as artfully designed *sets of relationships* that 'reflect the consequences of our actions back to us'.[8] Such artworks help you get a feeling for the tendencies flowing through the complexity that animates the world.

To deploy once again the ideas of engineer and philosopher Paul Cilliers, let's remember that 'complexity is diverse but organised' and 'descriptions of it cannot be reduced to simple, coherent and universally valid discourses'.[9] Complexity is not susceptible to precepts, therefore. To know a system, it is best to describe it in real time, if possible, in all its changefulness.

I am reminded here of a remarkable passage in the diaries of Samuel Taylor Coleridge, from his fieldnotes of 1803:

> Thursday Morning, 40 minutes past One o'clock - a perfect calm - now & then a breeze shakes the heads of the two Poplars, [& disturbs] the murmur of the moonlight Greta, then in almost a direct Line from the moon to me is all silver- Motion and Wrinkle & light - & under the arch of the Bridge a wave ever & anon leaps up in Light … silver mirror/ gleaming of moonlight Reeds beyond–as the moon sets the water from Silver becomes a rich yellow. - Sadly do I need to

have my Imagination enriched with appropriate Images for Shapes-/Read Architecture, & Icthyology.[10]

Here we see Coleridge immersed and finally overwhelmed by the details of the lively world; we see him yearning but ill-equipped to understand the entirety, to know the shapes, the semantics of the full and fluctuating scene that washes over him. Even as he knows it is futile to try to catch the full and wondrous intricacy of an emerging moment, he affirms that description with whatever means available – in his case in language, in modern cases it might be with microphones an cameras – *description* is the best chance he has of intellectually grasping the multi-sensory abundance of all that is going on around and within him in any dynamic moment of worldly experience.

This recalls Cilliers' axiom that 'to describe a system you have … to *repeat* the system'.[11] You cannot reduce a complex circumstance to a simplified model or to stabilised schematics, because complexity is definitively dynamic, relationally intricate and always adjusting. You need to *experience* a complex circumstance, to be with its changes through time, to feel its shifts whilst also being attuned to the historically determined tendencies and the feedback patterns of stimuli and responses that are organising it from myriad perspectives at any particular moment. Or to reprise Cilliers:

> complex systems have to grapple with a changing environment. … To cope with these demands the system must have two capabilities: it must be able to store information concerning the environment for future use; and it must be able to adapt … when necessary.[12]

In traditional artforms, the artist often conjures an impression of complexity either by manipulating absences or inserting deliberate contradictions which goad the perceiver's imagination. In literature or in painting, for instance, the adaptability and complexity occur symbolically in a 'space' between the perceiver's self and the artwork, in the strummed intellect and memory and senses of the person engaging with the work at a particular instant. In more recent times, however, a new 'space' has become available. Digital-computational systems have been developed that enable an artwork itself – not just the relationship between the work and the perceiver – to transmogrify both in response to stimuli and at the behest of active and activating codes written into it. (It is not only artworks that do this now, of course. Most geo-located apps on your phone do something similar – incorporating your own motility into the ever-updating environment that you and the geo-spatial system are observing and mapping and composing together.) In such artworks a comprehensive aesthetic dimension is always added as the adaptability and complexity are found always emerging *in the work* as well as in the imaginative 'space' between the perceiver and the work. Rather than being implicit and always somewhat opaque inside the ruminations of each perceiver encountering an object 'over there', with an interactive-immersive environment the complex of relationships and repercussions that get activated by the perceiver's engagement can now also be shown to be explicitly altering the work itself. The 'feedback' involving initiative and repercussion is usually instantaneous. And it is dramatically ecological in the way it shows the interactor the ramifications of so much recursivity, of so much inter-dependence and enmeshment between 'self' and 'others'.

The drive to understand the dynamics of what Cilliers calls 'constrained diversity' appears to be strengthening in contemporary culture.¹³ Which brings us to the nub of Cilliers' thesis about the most effective way to know complexity. You have to get inside the system, narrate what is going on, then narrate again and again, from as many vantage-points in space and time as possible. (Note how similar this is to Coleridge's sense that he needs to be here, there and everywhere, with increased speeds of perception and various modes of apperception, in order to gain a fuller appreciation of any phenomenon.) You do all this in order to get an eventual and eventful feeling for the way the system is tending.

As mentioned in previous chapters of this book, Cilliers helps us understand how 'complex systems are open systems'. Their constituent parts (including yourself, if you are amidst them) and their observable actions all change from moment to moment, which means often 'the very distinction between "inside" and "outside" the system becomes problematic'.¹⁴ Complexity is not especially tractable to analysis, therefore, because the 'object' under analysis is altering from moment to moment. Indeed, it is not an object. It is an event, an experience, a shifting set of relationships. Because you are in it and causing some of its characteristics, the system is not separate from your subjective, appreciative self. Critical distance is not available.

In other words, there is a network that engulfs you rather than an object that addresses you. If you try to map those relationships as an active network, 'any given narrative will form a path, or trajectory, through the network. … [and as you] trace various narrative paths through it, it changes.¹⁵ If you were to 'cut up' a complex system, you would find that your 'analytical method destroys what it seeks to understand'.¹⁶

Thus we first need to treat all discernible patterns as momentary, contingent sets of provisional principles (albeit principles governed by some abiding code or algorithm that is always giving rise to the system); next we have to take those principles *into* the meretricious environment, so as to assay their validity and influence, knowing that the principles will eventually fail or need adjustment. Once we sense those failures and adjustments registering in our analytical faculties we are set apart again, organizing another speculative batch of contingent principles which we must then take back into the system. Inside but outside but inside but outside but inside. It is a rhythm that is restless but necessary, *because the world of lived experience is not simple, static or stable.* Not functionally objective, as Aristotelian and Cartesian approaches presume (and effectively require) it to be.

### The Artwork – inside and outside 'Street X-Rays'

It is a rhythm I have tried to encourage in 'Street X-Rays'. The installation makes a clearing, I hope. It makes a clearing not in a forest literally, but in a kind of urban jungle, in a space and time where past and present desires and anxieties are forever shaping and altering existence in a city which we inhabit even as we reflect on it.

Featuring a collection of crime-scene photographs from the 1950s, adding contemporary video cityscapes plus enigmatic texts composed as a response to police reports, 'Street X-Rays' is a projection-and-sound environment that shows the past and the present living and moving in each other in much the same way that we live and move in our taken-for-granted habitats and timescales.

The visitor enters an 8-metre-by-8-metre darkened vault and encounters a loose 'labyrinth' of five projected screens floating in darkness. Each screen carries a diptych displaying the present alongside the past. Encountering an eerie batch of locations photographed by forensic investigators in Sydney between 1945 and 1955, we re-visit the exact spots where the images were originally captured. Now a video and sound sequence has been recorded, thus providing the raw materials for the basic components of the project: five diptych screens with stereo sound, each one fed by a video projector. The left-hand side of each screen shows the original black & white police picture. The right-hand side shows the contemporary video footage.

For each video cityscape, the positioning of the camera, its static framing and its lens specifications replicate those in the original photograph. We go back to the exact place where some criminal event tore the world for a period of time. The modern-day sound is captured too. And the light, colour and décor of the present-day scene always set the video sequences in dialogue with the original. (The live location sound from the video mingles with an algorithmic music composition by Greg White and Chris Abrahams.)

On each screen after a while, a diptych fades to black. Then a caption-title fades up. Once this caption has been on screen for a short period, its associated next diptych appears on the screen as the caption fades away.

Out of phase with each other, all five screens go through an endless relational re-alignment of sound to image to text across the intricate spatial array of the installation.

The caption texts work as follows. Before the appearance of the relevant images, we see a short text detailing the original crime. Examples of caption-titles:

>  Death by Misadventure
>  Frequenting a Disorderly House
>  Malfeasance with a Motor Vehicle
>  Expose, Harass & Defile
>  Man lurking in a yard

The texts turn to 'mirror-writing' toward the end of the duration of their appearance; this allows the text to be readable on either side (back-projection or front-projection) of the floating screen; it also adds a kind of temporal urgency or 'deadline' to the interpretation of each diptych sequence. Once the inter-title has faded away, a new image-diptych fades up. And so on.

Also, after the presentation of five or six diptychs on any particular screen , there is a lengthy text that holds on the screen for 30 seconds or more. The entire exhibit contains ten of these texts, which would be revealed over a period of 12 minutes or so. Examples:

The following facts are true of this city:

It's a place you know well. It's larger than Valparaiso. Warmer than Vladivostok. More water than Cairo. With no distinctive accent, not like Boston or Cardiff. Less concerned about finance than Chicago or Brussels. Overrun by sailors at fortnightly intervals. Recovering from war.

These types of rain occur in the city:

Cutting – sandy – the size of a coin – smelling of sleep – with a rhythm that's Cuban – like England – like Idaho – the contents of a saucepan flicked across a room – warm as the blood of a chicken – like a sentence in prison – helpful when moderate.

These phrases were found in the notebook of a mortician who died on a train:

## A Forest. A Clearing.

Some by fire. Some by water. An electrical appliance. Opiates. Gunshot. The front of the hand. The back of the hand. A man in a rage. A man full of shame. Often metal is involved. Some are marked by speed. No breakage of skin. (But this is rare.) Or … slow and in night-time. (This is quite frequent.)

The screens are translucent enough to allow a 'palimpsest' of the imagery to get cast out through the diaphanous scrim over to the walls of the gallery, thus making a faintly vertiginous impression as the washed out scenes careen around the room in much the same away the sound does, even as the screens also anchor the room with 'stations' of crisp, bright imagery calling on the attention of the participant-observer.

These screens themselves are arranged so that the visitor never sees all the gallery's imagery from any one vantage-point. Moreover the visitor's silhouetted presence is always poised to cast a shadow onto one or more screens as the participant-observer enters the full, explore-able scene. This spatial arrangement of the main features of the artwork is somewhat similar, in an admittedly more banal fashion to the way the stones are placed in the magnificent Zen garden of Ryoan-Ji in Kyoto (which is one of the world's great and abiding changescapes): the viewer is always drawn on to a new perspective, to explore new stand-points without ever getting the impression that everything can be known in a single perception. A sense of one's endless insufficiency in encountering the plenitude of the world's experiences is a defining quality of 'Street X-Rays'. (Think again of Coleridge scribbling in his moonlit notebook.)

There is always more meditation to anticipate. There is always a vital portion of experience which has to be part-imagined and part-remembered rather than directly apprehended. And one is always aware of one's own presence in and impact on the delicate environment that gathers all around.

The combinative rhythms of the five-screen display and the minimal-but-immersing soundscape keep the entire installation emotionally and semantically 'alive' and intriguing. The moods and meanings of the work evolve as the various combinations of sound, image and text play out. The viewer is meant to feel as if they have wandered into the restless 'spirit history' of an unnamed but familiar city, as if its ordinary locations have come alive with historic traces and evocative charges that never go away but are usually below the limits of quick perception.

## Concluding Remarks

I have now detailed all the basic elements of the installation. To recap: a combination of the colourful moving images of today; the black&white still images of yesteryear; texts spurring enigmatic grabs of narratives; sounds interlacing to make symphony and occasional discord; movement disturbing your proprioception. All these elements combine so that the viewer can perceive the effects of time lingering in each scene and pulsing across the entire imaginative space of this half-historical/half-mythical city. The installation is a contemplative environment which highlights the endless patterned intricacy of urban history and metropolitan aesthetics.

Thus 'Street X-rays' is designed to be not only a meditation on the passing of time. The installation is also an inquest into the forces that shape and surge through our contemporary civic environments, the energies that push into the moods and sounds of our public spaces, the legacies, absences and persistent strengths lurking in our built environments. It is designed to be

## A Forest. A Clearing.

a deliberately *immersive* and *investigative* zone, a dynamic model of urbanism, amnesia and custodial narrative, a dynamic model that encourages the forensic, skeptical and restless engagement of the visitor. It's a clearing that affords visitors a chance to contemplate the effects of their own presence in an environment that's replete with remnant momentum suffusing its present dynamics.

So, in the final analysis, I have tried to conjure a place that is haunted by persistent little pulses of history, in the hope that visitors get a feeling that they've wandered into a vaguely familiar 'otherworld' that is being buffeted by a kind of 'spirit weather'. It is meant to be palpable, perceptible but somewhat ineffable, to be known through immersion but also and simultaneously through reflection. Like a clearing in a forest.

### Notes

1   'Street X-Rays' is part of a larger suite of works (collectively known as 'Life After Wartime') which draws on the NSW Police Department's photographic archive at the Justice & Police Museum in Sydney. 'Life After Wartime' is a continuing collaboration (1998–2015) with Kate Richards and an ensemble of artists, including Greg White, Aaron Seymour and Chris Abrahams. (See www.lifeafterwartime.com) 'Street X-Rays' was first installed as part of the exhibition. 'PROOF: the act of seeing with one's own eyes' at the Australian Centre for the Moving Image, November 2004–February 2005. It was an outcome of a Linkage Project Grant from the Australian Research Council, in partnership with the Australian Centre for the Moving Image, which now owns a copy of the work in its collection.

### Credits
Writing, Design, Direction – Ross Gibson.
Cinematography – Ben Speth.
Sound – Chris Abrahams and Greg White.
Fabrication – Lenny Bastiaans.
Special Thanks – Kathryn Bird, Kate Richards, Ricky Subritzky, UTS, ACMI.
Technical Specifications of 'Street X-Rays'

5 DVDs or media players plus algorithmic, evolutionary soundtrack on two channels plus stereo location sounds, plus five translucent, suspended projection screens with an enclosed gallery.

2   Celsus Kelly (editor and translator), *La Austrialia del Espiritu Santo: the journal of Fray Martin de Munilla O.F.M. and other documents relating to the Voyage of Pedro Fernandez de Quiros to the South Sea (1605–1606) and the Franciscan Missionary Plan (1617–1627)*, volume one, Hakluyt Society, Cambridge: The University Press, 1966, p. 117.
3   O.H.K. Spate, *The Pacific Since Magellan. Volume One: the Spanish lake*, London: Croom Helm, 1979, p.137.
4   'Unmapped' and 'uncharted' are necessarily contentious terms. Indigenous sailors knew these seas well and although they never produced 'charts', they did remember star patterns and accounts of master-navigators' experiences; and they did carry twig assemblages that helped them recall wind patterns and currents and that could validly be called 'maps'. It was the incursive sailors, not the incumbent ones, who felt the seas were 'unmapped'.
5   Frederick Garber, *Thoreau's Redemptive Imagination*, New York: New York University Press, 1977, p.2.
6   Garber, p.2.
7   Garber, p.11.
8   David Rokeby, 'Transforming Mirrors: subjectivity and control in interactive media', in Simon Penny (ed.), *Critical Issues in Electronic Media*, State University of New York Press, Albany, 1995, p. 152.
9   Paul Cilliers, *Complexity and Postmodernism*, London: Routledge, 1998, p. 130.
10  Quoted in Patricia S. Yaeger, 'Coleridge, Derrida, and the Anguish of Writing', in *SubStance*, vol. 12, no. 2, issue 39 (1983), p. 91.
11  Cilliers, pp. 130 and 10 respectively.
12  Cilliers, p. 10.
13  Cilliers, p. 127.
14  Cilliers, p. 99.
15  Cilliers, p. 130.
16  Cilliers, p. 2.

## 14

## MOTILITY

In January 1788, on the eastern edge of the landmass that would eventually become known as Australia, the colonising English militia established their first beachhead on the swampy strand of Botany Bay. Momentous as it might have seemed while it was happening, this foundational act proved to be just a flitting instance. Within a couple of days, Commander Arthur Phillip decided the garrison had to relocate to better shelter. This required a tricky sail around imposing headlands to investigate a hunch that had been dropped into a ship's log two decades earlier, when Captain James Cook had mentioned coasting past an alluring inlet as he had headed north during the famous voyage of 1769–70.

Good luck shone on Phillip's fleet in this speculative move, for the ships tacked into one of the world's finest deep harbours and soon they were anchored in a temperate freshwater cove where the modern metropolis of Sydney now thrums. In retrospect, however, when we look past the manifest destiny that seems to shine in this tale about the 'discovery' of Sydney Harbour, we can see another moral in the story: even as the marines initiated the colony, settler Australia glimpsed, but failed to register, that there is something fluid inherent to existence in this country. The tale of relocation intimates how settlement is provisional in this place, how one has to be ready always to keep moving.

The need for so much responsiveness would not have been surprising to the newcomers if they had been able to hold their minds open to fresh understanding. For the indigenes thronging the cove were water people—improvisatory, opportunistic and weather-guided—who canoed purposefully back and forth across the choppy harbour and up and down the long reaches of tidewater. But a countervailing fixity of mind governed—and continues to organise—the English settlement. Straight away, for example, the colonists locked themselves in place by staking perpetual claims to the land they seized, inaugurating the cadastral property deeds that tether bounded plots of country to particular individuals. This system of sequestering ownership – this 'real estate' – is still a mainstay of the national economy.

As the decades have accrued, though, the colonial fixity has never fully gelled. For even though the land itself seems to be the rock-solid basis of Australian experience, the defining quality here is actually *changefulness*. There's a motility in Australia—something skittish, relational and ever-altering—which means long-term inhabitants should expect only occasional moments of poise while remaining always engaged in jostling contingency and fragility. History teaches that to live well here, you need to be scanning close and far, catching environmental instructions, ready to respond when each emerging moment brings a new pulse of threats and chances. This requires a mentality that is attentive to the environment but not deeply embedded in any one locked and landed portion of it.

The fluidity that is indigenous to Australia—in the original people and the environment—has proven so complex and all-encompassing that it has persistently flummoxed many presumptions of settler Australia, thwarting the newcomers' regularly reiterated and evermore repercussive attempts to establish landholding dynasties of profitable agriculture and mining. Across several generations, settlers thought it natural to expect a livelihood based either on grounded and consistently repeating cycles of annual harvest, or on the extraction of purportedly inexhaustible 'primary resources' such as mineral ores and fossil fuels.

A quick way to intuit how the settler-fantasy of fixity has always been countervailed by endemic fluidity is to recall something obvious but often overlooked: Australia is at the southeastern extremity of Asia, which is philosophically unified, despite its immense cultural and geographical variety, around the stopless 'S' that writhes serpentine in its middle. (I recall hearing a radio interview with Michael Ondaatje, at least twenty years ago, in which he made this point.) Plus: Australia is amidst the Pacific and Indian Oceans. It is in the restless, watery part of the world. Indeed, it is evermore intensively populated by migrants who know these waters. Furthermore, even amongst those Indigenous Australians whose ways derive not from the harbour reaches but from desert zones, from places nowhere near vast draughts of water, even these peoples' traditional behaviours are shaped by fluid kinds of mentalities, given how the desert cultures take their improvisational cues from the shifting weather and seasons, from the blooming and shrinking of botany, from runs of wind and rain and fire and animal migrations. Country-defined and water-frugal as they are, even these desert people are oceanic within the massed tracts of country that they serve.

Into this national dynamic, during the past two centuries, generation after generation of newcomers have tangled. As new characteristics of Australian society keep emerging, there is no end to the influx from without, and thus there is no stanching the flux within the ever-altering settlement. So it is pointless, really, to keep insisting that 'settlement' is a valid description or aspiration for the postcolonial and globalised enterprise that is contemporary Australia.

An increasing number of artists have begun to examine this paradox. Simryn Gill is preeminent among these questers and questioners. In decades of work, interweaving her insights and influences from Sydney, Malaysia and the Indian diaspora—in all of which she has spent significant time—Gill has redefined the commonsense understanding of everyday experience in the Australian Commonwealth. This is not all she has done, for her work has aesthetic, philosophical and ritual concerns that extend beyond the national topic. But as I restrict myself just to the theme of parochial identity in this instance (because Gill has recently been spotlighted as the national representative for the international biennial art exposition in Venice) I am struck by how radically she has renovated a notion that has long been considered axiomatic: the notion that an examination of Australian experience must focus principally on the ways we understand *place,* on the ways one is meant, eventually, to feel *grounded* when one defines oneself, privately or publicly, as Australian.

Gill's work brings a revelation to the place-anchored debates about Australian experience. She suggests, implicitly and enigmatically rather than explicitly or simply, that to be Australian might have less to do with being in a place than it has to do with being in temporal patterns of movement, being in rhythms of only gleaming realisation, being in glimpsed insights and occluding befuddlements, in a continual process of reorientation, action and reaction. Gill helps us sense how being Australian might actually mean being untethered or placeless. It might mean being blithely restless within the changefulness that the nation offers its citizens, which means appreciating how to live in dynamic patterns of time rather than principally in native plots of place.

To explain this puzzle concerning national 'timeliness', I need to spend a few more sentences examining the history of Australian 'placedness'.

Until recently, across the twenty-three decades of colonisation, the quest to define 'Australian identity' has been a quest to know fulfilling settlement ('fulfilling' has spiritual as well as material connotations). This idea has long been a commonplace, the notion that the land is what makes the nation special. As this commonsense idea has taken hold, Indigenous and incursive cultures equally have accepted the proposition that in order to be or to become Australian, in order to feel 'at home' here, a prospective citizen needs to develop a sustained, sustainable and sustaining relationship to the land. According to this logic, the land distinguishes us internationally while it unites us nationally; the land is our grounding, our home base, our special haven, and store of resilience.

With the value of place seeming so self-evident in Australia, the main debate has usually been around how best to attain this grounded sense of belonging. There have been three standard ways to summon this feeling. First, 'progressive' commentators have customarily accepted that the most compelling accounts of placement come from the Indigenous people, who are defined by their ancient tales of *arising* from the land. The Indigenous people are the autochthonous ones. They are *of* the land and they set the standard for entrenched and earned knowledge of how to be in this place over long stretches—*millennial* stretches—of time. Second, there have been the settlers, the invaders, the colonists, the immigrants, the refugees, all of whom have stories not of arising but of *arriving*. Political contexts, as much as factual accounting, determine how these newcomers are accorded meanings through stories of how these people came to be in this place after leaving somewhere else, stories that can serve to justify their case for staying in their new home, if the tales are judged reliable and worthy or uplifting enough. Then there's the third type: settlers' heirs who are native-born and on a quest to believe that they have legitimately arisen from their home-place in new, non-Aboriginal ways. Blessed or cursed with a shallow autocthony.

For a long time, these three types of placeholding shaped all discussions about citizenship in Australia. Debate focused on the different degrees of arising and arriving in a citizen's legacy. Every prospective citizen had to face up to the definitive questions: where did you come from, and how deeply do your experiences and attitudes now constitute roots that attach you to your island home? There were many differences of opinion and privilege operating in this interrogation, but for all the divisiveness—as well as the inclusiveness of state-endorsed multiculturalism—the definitions of citizenship were always unified around an axiomatic acceptance of the primacy of place in Australian identity.

This has changed with the arriving of Pacific Islanders and Asians, as already mentioned, and with the arising of a new phalanx of people principally valuing their sexuality, for example, or the connectivity and protean vitality of their many networked affinity-groups above their nationality. These latter groups define themselves according to the ways they can actively drift and shift and continue to alter within a wide and fluid world of communicated opportunities, rather than according to how quickly and deeply they can settle and pledge steadfastness to a constrained set of verities tagged to landscapes and neighbourhoods.

Without being a spokeswoman for these proliferating generations, Gill fashions a way to be in, of and across contemporary Australia by imagining it as an ever-evolving nation that is principally a contentious, unstinting *event,* tangled in a plethora of life-cycles of burgeon and decay that are not only organic but also psychological and sociological. For Gill, the nation is not a place with fundamental qualities that need to be unearthed and absorbed. Rather, it is a conjunction of influences and occurrences moving in time within space. The nation is comprised of cycles of historical, natural, physical, personal, and political action and repercussion that are all emerging and submerging, implicating and explicating, combining and contending in matter, in ecologies, in individual psychologies, in families, in communities and in an array of sub-societies that work their changes on each other within the national and international economies that are operating here and now.

This nation is therefore anything but stable. Anything but singular. Its cycles of changefulness range from the diurnal through to the millennial. It is guided not cardinally by simple, eternal ideals or essences. It is always in process, evolving and devolving, but somehow cohering like a complex system as culture gives form and continuity to the contingencies of experience in interaction with human action, some of it intended, some of it guided, much of it unknowing.

This is why an exhibition by Gill is never a collection of finely-finished products. Rather, it is a slow-entropy event—something in process and unsettling—wherein the host environment of the gallery alters through time, as do the displayed things that one might have expected to be cosseted as *objets d'art*.

Most dramatically, in the Australian Pavilion at the Venice Biennale, the roof was breached and a large portion of the protective canopy was removed so that the weather was let in to do its expressive work on the building's interior and on the exhibition's various artifacts that have been offered to time amidst the natural elements. (Gill had discovered that the building was being decommissioned after the Biennale, to be replaced in the near future by an entirely new gallery. What could be more suited to her thematics!) Simple nationalist values were tricked out and troubled in this exhibition. For example, consider the photographs that Gill installed and offered up for decay. At first glance, the pictures appeared to be traditionally Australian, apparently grounded with that old place-obsessed essentialism. Sumptuous large format photographs of country, they looked like grand landscape ventures in the tradition of the many male painters—examples from a long list include Sidney Nolan, Fred Williams, John Coburn and Tim Storrier—who have been installed as national treasures after offering the public a trove of place-pictures that *seem* to reveal some land-steeped vision of eternal and essential Australian-ness. In these men's essence-scapes, there is usually some nationalist gist. The gist is always oblique, sublime or mystified somewhat, offered but made procedurally enigmatic, as if the artist has broken through to know the *genius loci* but the medium will not show it easily to just anybody. In this dramaturgy, the artist is the repository of the putative truth, not the artwork.

Gill's landscape photographs – which are actually photographs shot by her from an aeroplane cruising above the sites of open-cut mines – seem similar to such treasures. But they are different.

On first inspection, Gill's minescapes appear to place her in the heroic tradition of Nolan, Williams, et al. The pictures seem to offer images of raw country that will be smelted down to wealth once the crude ores have been scooped from the ancient ground. But the minescapes are in fact several artworks at once. They are not finished products; they are in-process records of the continuing event of Gill's environmental attentiveness. Not celebrations of essence-extraction, in fact they show and help us understand a little more about the energetically acquisitive activity that is so often sunk, over extended durations of prospective exploitation, into postcolonial country in Australia.

Always in the process of becoming some different artwork, Gill's photographs are evocations of a nimble, changeful mentality, insofar as they allow the viewer to hover and appreciate the scene before *moving on* in cogitation. They are snapshotted reports from an unresting patrol over a vast, mercurial country that can be known only in its connectivity, only in momentarily apprehended scenes that are always attached to a constellation of other evolving event-scenes. These are pictures that do not invest in any single, locked-off place. Instead, they push the mind out to the vast networks, not only of global economics, but also of the interconnected ecological vitality that maintains a not-entirely-knowable cogency in the land. This latter cogency is no single thing, no essence to be captured; rather it is an active, ever-altering system of eventualities and connectivities activating over time.

If I had been asked to write the wall-sheet for these pictures in the roofless pavilion, I would have gone to the library and transcribed Percy Shelley's famous sonnet, and felt no need to say more:

'Ozymandias'

I met a traveller from an antique land
Who said: Two vast and trunkless legs of stone
Stand in the desert…Near them, on the sand,
Half sunk, a shattered visage lies, whose frown,
And wrinkled lip, and sneer of cold command,
Tell that its sculptor well those passions read
Which yet survive, stamped on these lifeless things,
The hand that mocked them, and the heart that fed:

And on the pedestal these words appear:
'My name is Ozymandias, king of kings:
Look on my works, ye Mighty, and despair!'
Nothing beside remains. Round the decay
Of that colossal wreck, boundless and bare
The lone and level sands stretch far away.[1]

Artworks like Gill's, which are concerned with changefulness in Australia, tend to be processes, not products, not distilled concentrates of conclusive insight. They rarely achieve a stasis that has to be conserved. Instead, they move our mentality in a connective drift across time and space, seeking engagement with the ever-emerging, systematic animus of the country and its protean society. To conclude, just for this moment, let's say that Gill's work is concerned not with the secured object, therefore, but with the motile event or changescape that is contemporary Australia.

**Notes**

1 Percy Bysshe Shelley, 'Ozymandias' in *The Complete Poetical Works of Percy Bysshe Shelley (Volume 1)*. This edition has been made available online via Project Gutenberg: https://www.gutenberg.org/cache/epub/4800/pg4800.html , accessed 20-12-2014.

## 15

## DEEP WATER TIME

Astonishment. Quick shifts of consciousness. Startling changes in perspective. Generating such jolts, the contemporary Chinese artist Cai Guo-Qiang has always striven to startle. His chosen role: revelator.

Hence his devotion to the transformative energy that zings through the medical sciences of the Chinese ancients; hence his enthusiasm for the kinetic flourishes that enliven the best calligraphy; hence his exhilaration with the geomantic verve of feng shui; also, the bright detonation of gunpowder. Cai's mission, stated simply, is to focus your intensity, drawing vivid images to prominence and pushing obfuscation away. 'I have a lot of curiosity,' he has observed, 'about unseen force and invisible things'.[1] Always looking to expose the concealed urges that give form to our full, befuddling world, he works to make the inscrutable imaginable.

There is no denying that Cai's projects tend to be spectacular. He brings the WOW Factor. Extending the Great Wall of China with a blazing lateral flare, for example, or composing a massive metallic freeze-frame that permanently levitates the lethal starburst of a terrorist's car-bomb, Cai can seem a modern-day P T Barnum, generating hoopla with a bold imagination empowered by his far-reaching celebrity. Belying his courtesy and courtliness, he can appear paradoxically like some mountebank trickster, or a global magician. What to make of this enigmatic shimmer about him? This magic?

To go deeper, let's define 'magic' as a set of ingenious techniques finessed by an expert who wants to shift the observer's mindset from blunt scepticism to whetted wonderment. Now let's propose that Cai practices an artful magic. This helps us see better how determinedly and methodically he works to spritz common sense and to give the dull world a little galvanising dazzle.

With the magic, he always tries to be as illuminating as thrilling. Sometimes he is chilling too, as in the example of the car-bombs, where he proposes that you suspend judgement for a cooling moment so you can really look into this abomination, really try to understand the animus within it. He rattles the lenses through which you habitually interpret everyday experience, kicking in some new light so that, at least for a little while after he's brought the astonishment, you have to wonder about those invisible things and the unseen force underneath the evident things. He offers new vantages on the mundane.

'Mundane' means literally 'of the world'. It can be used as a synonym, of course, for 'ordinary'. Cai's works are always of the world, but they are set invariably at a provocative angle to the ordinary. For the deep codes concealed beneath the world's surfaces are anything but mundane. The word 'other-worldly' comes to mind. Investigating the likelihood that something wondrous subtends mundanity: with this open-ness to mystery, Cai goes to work.

Try an experiment. Imagine a world where any one of these notions – the mystical, the political or the magical – necessarily contains the other two. Now think of an artist seeking revelations in such a world. This brings you closer to grasping Cai's enterprise. This is what makes him much more than a trickster. As he delves into everything that is present but not obvious (seeking how 'to go beyond social systems and boundaries', as he puts it), Cai says candidly that he is trying to 'time travel'[2]. He lures next and past moments into the present — or more precisely he lures them *into the present imagination of you the appreciator* — so that all the histories and future possibilities in matter and moments might be apprehensible as part of the ever-emerging instant that is now.

To grasp Cai's enthusiasm for time-shifting, consider his 'Projects for Extraterrestrials', the enormous, gunpowder-fuelled chain-reacting explosions that he staged all round the world throughout the 1990s. During this fin-de-siecle era, he delivered more than thirty of these logistically vast projects, equally thrilling and chilling in their beauty and violence. Each one, a scale-model apocalypse. (And each one, a kind of prototype for some of the more gorgeous sequences of mayhem in George Miller's mighty film, *Mad Max: Fury Road,* which is a project detonated with intelligence and flair commensurate with Cai's.)

Cai delivered time travel in the gunpowder. To illuminate his conception of time travel as a type of enhanced vision, let's assay the gunpowder itself. Something is poised — like a dragon, like thermo-dynamic urgency wanting to perform calligraphy — in the chemistry of this black-magical dust. In this earthy matter, the vivid future explosion is invisible, but present even as it is latent. At another moment in time, when the conditions are right, this exact same lax powder can flare to display its other brighter reality. *Time* brings this mystery to revelation; suddenly, almost all at once, time shifts and makes manifest everything forceful and full of potential that was lurking in the dull matter. Wrenching huge energy from elements extracted from the earth — in this way too gunpowder-art is 'extra-terrestrial' whilst also being so gigantic it can by viewed wholly only from outer space — each explosion is paroxysmic magic used for astonishing and befuddling us citizens lolling timeworn in mundanity.

When the gunpowder ignites, you can travel through time to see one of the more convulsive, invisible futures that might be stored up for the seemingly inert world. Then the clattering outburst settles down again and, in the aftermath, your memory carries both the dazzling detonation and the deceptively peaceable quietude that prevailed beforehand. From the gunpowder now, you have extracted other states, heretofore unrealised, *invisible* states. You have learned that change waits in all matter and moments.

The Chinese calligraphic mark for 'gunpowder' is translatable as 'fire-medicine'. With the application of good medicine, a skilled physician can alter dullness and lassitude till they become, in time, lustre and health. When a healthy balance prevails, each opposite state – illness and wellness – dwells in the other, much as yin and yang cosset each other. Viewed in a snapshot of simple, linear time, one state (such as illness) may occlude the other (such as wellness). But considered in the volumetric, active spirals of time that Cai envisages and investigates, all states of history are equally immanent and apprehensible. Which means the two opposite states – the dull and the bright – must dwell in a good medicine. And because, over the duration of an effective treatment, a good medicine draws the radiance out from the ailment, so a tincture or pulverised potion (often not much different in appearance from gunpowder) can be regarded as the fuel that serves a time traveller seeking better health.

Gunpowder can be such a potion for the body politic. For example, the 'Projects for Extraterrestrials'. Lasting more than a decade in their repeated detonations, and enduring for ever after in documentation, they have cajoled and jolted viewers to imagine that 'then', 'now' and 'the future' might all be living in each other, despite how different these tenses can seem when each is understood as a separate moment along one simple, straight timeline. Cai uses his gunpowder as a means of moving around in the past, present and future. Or more precisely, as a means of moving these tenses through each other and entangling them inseparably in each observer's consciousness. He helps us see how his fire-medicine, which appears so dull and inert when first brought to the scene, actually has brilliant, burning potentiality in it. This magical substance contains a state that was prepared previously, a state from another time that is actually already present and ready to emblazon your mind's eye when a coexistent time, a time poised and parallel with the present – namely, the time of its intended detonation – will be charged in your imagination even before it gets ignited in future physical space. Thus Cai helps the viewer know ubiquity in time, sensing all at once the wisdom of the ancients and the options of questers yet to come.

So how can we learn to live well with this knowledge that all times – the past, present and future – are always in each other? Here's one answer that's implied in most of Cai's work: via the imaginative ventures of culture, the dead can give us what we need for making our living if we refuse to allow the ancestors to fade into oblivion. In other words, we have to heed the energy of the invisible. We have to absorb the legacy of the past while enacting our most noble rituals so we can make sure that all those people and actions that have composed history can be activated again and again in the eternally unfolding now so they can 'serve the interests of the unborn'.[3] For example, consider how love works its magic in your family, or how the history of your tribe or community or nation might oblige you to keep the world healthy for the growing future, which will remember your past:

these are other ways to understand and access Cai's proliferative, all-at-once time.

Cai's artworks contend that invisibility can be made explicit in your imagination, just as a timeline can be revealed to be otherwise, to be nothing like a line in the way it presses all-at-once in folds and inter-penetrating meshes of causation and repercussion. Furthermore, even as multiple *times* overlay and interlace in Cai's work, his projects also cast us imaginatively and all at once into several distinct *places*. Thus the many vast craters of flame and outbursting energy that make up the full suite of 'Projects for Extraterrestrials'. As the title indicates, there are qualities in these explosions that are not visible to us groundlings; rather there are aspects of Cai's full, unfolding heat-events that can be seen and understood only from elsewhere. In Cai's massive magic tricks, some other *place* is always simultaneously and invisibly present, demanding acknowledgement, ready to press forward. You need to imagine yourself otherwise, literally as other to yourself, in some other time and place, in order to sense the full cohesion of Cai's energetic signals.

Cai grasped this 'simultaneity' during the first, challenging nine years that he ever spent 'elsewhere' (beginning in 1987) when he left his hometown in the Chinese Fujian Province to make a life in Japan. This was before the 'Projects for Extraterrestrials' brought him the fame and wherewithal to work at the grand, cosmic scale that now seems so effortless with him. In his early years in Japan, during his time of intensely productive alienation when, at first, little in his immediate environment seemed obvious or readily explicable, Cai began to see that China is always subtly inside Japan, and vice versa, and that the most significant factors of everyday experience are not necessarily the explicit ones. Once the more emphatic differences between the two places lost their impact, he began to plumb undercurrents and glimpse superimpositions, for example the similarities in practices of traditional medicine, or the emphasis on spirit flowing through all objects in the environment. In the 1980s, Japan was at the height of its technological futurism; and China was at the nadir, perhaps, of its late-Communist ossification. Yet Cai began to see how a rich and generative Chinese mundanity infuses Japan, present as a legacy of the infiltration of Ch'an Buddhism eight hundred years ago; and as a corollary, a Japanese kind of future also waits, along with many other possibilities, inside the Chinese present. Cai realised over time that unlike in Japan, 'the past fifty years in China have not created the stable conditions necessary for the modern Chinese to develop their own culture; there has been only turmoil'.[4] But the future from another place awaits in the present of his homeland. Seen in a larger, deeper scope of time, a changed China is available. And indeed, this has come to pass.

Or as Patrick White declaimed at the start of his magical-realist novel *The Solid Mandala*, (attributing the quote to the surrealist poet Paul Eluard): 'There is another world, but it is in this one'.[5] With his epigram, White insisted that the really vital other worlds are most likely *intra*terrestrial. This same intimation gleams in one of Cai's more recent works, 'Heritage', which was premiered to the world at the Gallery of Modern Art in Brisbane in the Australian summer of 2013/14.

During the development phase of 'Heritage', Cai declared that his recent explorations of Australia had brought him back to an avid commitment to the invisible energies of our brittle, spinning planet. He was clearly moved and changed by his encounter with the ancient, abiding resilience of special portions of Australian nature, particularly with the marvel that is the 'Blue Lake' on North Stradbroke Island, off the coast from Brisbane. Here Cai was thrilled and changed by a profound ecosystem which hydrologists estimate has maintained its dynamic and delicate balance of past-present-and-future fertility all through the last 7000 years.[6]

Equally, Cai was radically refocused by his encounters in the remarkable, polyglot experiment of recombinant ethnicity and mutable citizenship that is contemporary, multi-cultural Australia. He found in Australia a set of obligations and opportunities – natural and social – that had dropped out of sight for him, if indeed they had ever been evident, during his sojourns in China, Japan and America.

'Heritage' has an invisibility that is presently primed to explode in the near future, but in a manner exquisitely unlike the charge in Cai's extraterrestrial, gunpowder projects. Words strain to describe and evoke the impact of 'Heritage'. But here is a version: the viewer walks through a large doorway in the corner of huge, white enclosed space, as high as a basketball stadium and twice as wide and long. In the centre of the space, covering at least half the footprint (easily the size of two basketball courts) there is a vivid blue 'lake' of *almost* perfectly still liquid. The lake is roughly ovoid and surrounded, all the way out to the edges of the stadium, by fine sand, white and unperturbed by any marks, prints or debris. AND around the edges of the lake – around its entire circularity with narry a space at the verge – there are 99 full-sized animals, each and every one bending to drink from the liquid. These animals are breath-stoppingly life-like, as if warm but frozen in time. Tigers, bears, antelopes, kangaroos, lions, lambs and vulnerable foals. The beasts have been fashioned from artificial materials by expert artisans in China. They are not made by taxidermy, and somehow this *shows*. They do not carry the mien of death that taxidermy exudes; rather they embody a vitalist urge. You can sense the artisans' yearning to change dull matter into vivacity, to make each animal a metamorphosis in your imagination.

All this changes your heartbeat, thins your breathing and just about stops your thinking. You can feel every aperture in your senses adjusting to catch the significance of what you are perceiving. And after a minute or two with this amplified attentiveness, you hear then see then somehow feel and *smell* a tiny astonishment: every minute or so, a single drop of water exudes from the ceiling and plunges into the centre of the lake, startling with a loud, dolloped report and then massaging tender ripples out to the shoreline where each little wave caresses the lips of the stooping beasts.

Pad quietly into the hushed ambit of this bold, timid work. Note the sandy verge, mysteriously unmarked by any footprints of recent events. Or to say it another, more imaginative way: the sand is marked only by the generous fullness of *all time* in all its possibilities, not by the recent past-present, not by the evidence of just one layer from the non-linear enormity of history. Note also the paradoxical meniscus of the lake water. So replete is this vital liquid with a palpable tension spanning its surface. Yet so gentle is it too, so langourous and inviting with its subliminal undulations, caused by the subtlest seeping rhythm of time's tiniest pulse materialised in the form of that single expressed water-drop barely enlivening the lake surface from elsewhere, above, dripping again and again and again, like the heartbeat of the world. You can see how the tension and languor linger for each other in the liquid; they are implicit and invisibly available to each other, like China and Japan saturating each other, like the past, present and future lolling and cajoling and changing one another.

Now examine more intimately the great parliament of beasts that are girding the lake. The Babel of beasts. They are magically present – ubiquitous in time – in the unperturbed sand. See what a welter of different roles, past and future, these animals have in their assembled community. See how they are starvelings but they are also predators, and companions and collaborators. Plus, they are ambassadors of tolerance. And they are prey and dumb fodder. All these things at once. They are at home with each other even as they are estranged by inherited history and geography. See how they could explode *en masse*: if you behaved ineptly or provocatively while approaching them, they might scatter, they might panic and shed all their different species of blood in a gory calligraphic display that would festoon the waiting sand. See how they might tear the silence apart too, how they might obliterate the peaceable shoreline that sustains them. Imagine them eviscerating each other, or pulling *you* apart.

Next, imagine the several vaults of time that press all around this possibly centrifugal instant. See how many tensions could be sprung here that might obliterate the stillness. Imagine the jostling past that brought all these animal emissaries together to this hushed point in time and space. And imagine the next moment, when the paradoxically serene and mongrel gestalt of their assembly might disintegrate hugger-mugger.

With its suspension in mysterious timeliness, not timelessness, with its magically remade spatial setting, with the political commentary of its allegorical confederacy of heretofore-alienated participants, 'Heritage' continues Cai's explosive investigations of changefulness. We sense how the scene is primed to scatter out of its serenity into mayhem. But the explosion in 'Heritage' is whisper-quiet and in slow-motion. Or no-motion. And it is made with fire's opposite.

With this minimally undulating, aqueous installation Cai has become defter now and more grounded. He deploys a newly-calibrated attentiveness to the subtlest shifts in surfaces and timescales, and with it comes a fresh delicacy that brings him close to a sensibility so well evoked by the poet Rainer Maria Rilke, who proclaimed: 'We of the here and now are not for a moment hedged in the time-world, nor confined within it; we are incessantly flowing over and over to those who preceded us, to our origins and to those who seemingly come after us.' The physical world is just a portal to the moral world, and we are obliged to go deep, Rilke asserts, so we can know the debts, obligations and opportunities that are bequeathed to us by the world of time and matter that we have inherited. 'It is our task' Rilke continues, 'to imprint this temporary, perishable earth into ourselves so deeply, so painfully and passionately, that its essence can rise again 'invisibly' inside us … We are the bees of the invisible.'[7] We are the changescapers.

With the hushed poise of 'Heritage', Cai wafts a wonderment to the ground, a wonderment to match Rilke's yearning. This is an exciting new aspect of Cai's thrilling career. For inside his latest innovation there is also continuity. With 'Heritage' we see again the quarry that has been ever-present in Cai's work: *invisibility poised to let something appear.* It is there in the sand. In 'Heritage' we sense again, but with a new quietude and a grounded intensity this time, how it is actually the unseen – everything just outside the obvious frames of visible space and immediately present time – that informs and sustains us most subtly, most profoundly. We see how Cai has turned away from the extraterrestrials, seeking instead to divine the wellsprings of the sustaining earth that bears up underneath him and that still hosts us all despite the myriad vulnerabilities in today's troubled ecologies and political systems. We see how Cai has built a time-and-vision-machine for *intraterrestrials,* for questers devoted to the invisible urgencies that still run vivacity through the earth.

As we gather near Cai's quiet congress of animals, as we ponder the vital elements in the lake in the gallery, we are invited to tread carefully and knowledgably on the brittle ground, to approach the exquisite, vulnerable reservoir of time as if each one of us can feel and see how we have the chance either to consecrate or detonate this magically poised and primed earth that still offers us all its time. This place in time that still offers us the chances and obligations of change.

## Notes

1. Arthur Lubow, 'Cai Guo-Qiang: the pyrotechnic imagination', *New York Times Magazine*, 17 February 2008, quoted in David Elliott, 'Between Heaven and Earth: Space and Time in the Art of Cai Guo-Qiang', in *Cai Guo Qiang: Fallen Blossoms*, Philadelphia, Philadelphia Art Museum and The Fabric Workshop, 2010, p. 39.
2. Lubow in Elliott, p. 39.
3. Robert Pogue Harrison, *The Dominion of the Dead*, Chicago: The University of Chicago Press, 2003, p. ix.
4. Dana Friis-Hansen, Octavio Zaya & Serizawa Takashi, *Cai Guo-Qiang* London: Phaidon, 2002, p.19.
5. Patrick White, *The Solid Mandala*, London: Eyre & Spottiswoode, 1966, Frontispiece.
6. See the ABC Radio report on the work of Dr Cameron Barr from the University of Adelaide: http://www.abc.net.au/news/2013-06-04/adelaide-researchers-find-remarkable-little-changed-lake-in-que/4732122. See also: http://www.adelaide.edu.au/news/news61741.html
7. Rainer Maria Rilke, *Letters of Rainer Maria Rilke (Volume Two, 1910–1926 )*, translated by Jane Bannard Greene and M.D. Herter Norton, New York: W. Norton & Co, 1st edition, 1948, pp. 373–74.

# ACKNOWLEDGMENTS

The writing in this book has been sustained by an academic culture, mainly in Australia but also reaching out to the rest of the world, that is dedicated to the rigorous review and encouragement of everyday culture and the work of imaginative thinking. Because of the strictures and the sense of obligation and responsibility pressing upon everyone working in this context, you could call the culture an economy, so long as you realise how much dedication and generosity goes into it, dedication and generosity beyond the simple measures and evaluation of economic accounting.

I am indebted to many people, institutions and publications for their support, especially for the editorial improvement and dissemination of early drafts of many chapters in this book. I acknowledge and thank them here. If I have missed anyone, the error is inadvertent and the gratitude abides.

Versions of chapters appeared in the following publishing entities:

Australia Council for the Arts (Publications Unit)
Continuum Journal
Cultural Studies Review
GOMA at the Queensland Art Gallery (Publications Unit)
IDEA Journal  (Interior Design and Interior Architecture)
IM Online Journal

Interventions Journal
Journal of Australian Studies
Postcolonial Studies Journal
Sydney University Press
TEXT Journal
University of Melbourne Publishing
University of Western Australia Publishing

I owe special thanks to the following people:

Suzi Attiwill
Geoffrey Batchen
Liz Conor
Ann Elias
Ross Harley
Gini Lee
Scott McQuire
Nikos Papastergiadis
Jennifer Rutherford
Lee Wallace
Jen Webb
Elizabeth Webby
Terri-ann White

Most of all, as always, I thank Kathryn Bird.

www.ingramcontent.com/pod-product-compliance
Lightning Source LLC
Chambersburg PA
CBHW020637220526
45464CB00001B/190